"The best nature writer working in Britain today."
David Craig, *Los Angeles Times*

"Glowing and compelling." *Countryman*

"Truly exquisite; every sentence is a delight … Crumley's
expertise never dulls his curiosity … Keen-eyed, careful and
companionable, he is the best guide I know to the natural
world." Malachy Tallach

"Breathtaking … moments of close observation, immersion
and poetry … a delight." *BBC Wildlife Magazine*

"Combines an extraordinary depth of detailed, recorded
knowledge with vivid warm writing … enchanting." Sara
Maitland, *BBC Countryfile Magazine*

"Powerful…deeply moving…The whole is a cornucopia
of autumnal delight." Polly Pullar, *The Scots Magazine*

"Connoisseurs of nature and good writing will be
enthralled by his first-person wildlife encounters …
written with dazzling clarity, lyrical tilt and a story-teller's
skill." *BBC Countryfile Magazine*, Book of the Month

"All luminous moments, small delights and bright
meditations drawn from the northern cold … invites us
to linger a while and witness frosty gifts made vivid by the
warmth of his conversation." Miriam Darlington

"Crumley has earned himself the enviable position of our
foremost nature commentator … Meditative … bewitching
… outspoken … persuasive … a true winter's tale." *Herald*

"Crumley conveys the wonder of the natural world at its
wildest…with honesty and passion and, yes, poetry." Susan
Mansfield, *Scottish Review of Books*

Lakeland Wild

Jim Crumley

Saraband

Published by Saraband
Digital World Centre, 1 Lowry Plaza,
The Quays, Salford, M50 3UB
www.saraband.net

ISBN: 9781913393212
ebook: 9781913393229

Printed and bound in Great Britain by Clays Ltd, Elcograf S.p.A.

1 2 3 4 5 6 7 8 9 10

Cover image: 'Quenched Summer', 2020, by Tessa Kennedy,
contemporary landscape artist.

Contents

1 Nowhere under the Rainbow............................1

2 The Tree Mountaineers (1) 13

3 Nature's Social Union 27

4 The Tree Mountaineers (2)..........................47

5 The Juniper Belt.......................................79

6 Time Stalls, You Grow Still, You Go Deeper In ..97

7 A Sense of Place Fell 121

8 Golden Eagle, Silver Swan...........................133

9 A Sense of Rightness Regained.....................155

10 Ash to Ashes 183

11 Divining in Reverse 191

   Acknowledgements 209

Remember Well

Keith Graham

1932–2020

One

Nowhere under the Rainbow

Lakeland Omens

No one likes to be a fish
out of water, least of all
the fish. In a land not named
by my native tongue the words
are awkward; I reach
for the solace, the embrace,
of my life's very rock,
and hold on. And bolder
then the beauty
I need begins to seed in me,
to feed me, to read me
the runes of this southern airt
that calls itself "The North"
and then calls forth
a peregrine and flings a rainbow
between High Rigg and the rest
of the world, for they know
— the beauty, the land —
that these I understand.

OMENS. SOMETIMES THEY CATCH in my throat. Take peregrines. It isn't always speed with peregrines. Sometimes it's guile and glide, the grace that allies rock-shaded plumage to a rock-thirled life, the shallow-angled entrance from crag-dark shadow into sunlight so that it's suddenly *there*, a presence that startles because you never saw it coming, never saw the shadowed release from the eyrie among the highest rocks (always the highest rocks, peregrines make more use of air than most). Now watch. The glide levels out and then tilts upwards on the command of three wingbeats, an equally shallow climb. All that is required for the moment is momentum, for the falcon has the all-seeing eyes of the gods, and the objective at the end of the manoeuvre is far off and beyond the grasp of your eyesight and mine. Bird brain: invariably we use the expression as a put-down, but this…this is the opening gambit of bird chess, and behold, it is a thing of beauty.

This is the peregrine falcon I carry with me in my head, this grand master of a bird; and 200 miles to the south of my comfort zone, just when I needed a reinforcing nod of recognition from nature, I was about to discover that it was waiting in the wings.

Omens. They drift across the face of the Earth like wind-blown spores. And I tend to incline towards those spores that only create something new when they fuse unexpectedly with another spore. There is no telling their landfall, science cannot plot their course, so what chance does a nature writer have, travelling more in hope than expectation? Yet when you work every day with two such mercurial life forces as nature and the creative arts, and if you live and breathe by the grace of your diplomatic skills' capacity to persuade them to align in common cause, then good omens are lifebelts. You reach out, you cling on, you try not to drown.

All the way up High Rigg, then, I scanned the wind for omens, for ways of tuning in, for one fortuitous spore that might overwhelm the odds and fuse with a restless spore from over the border, and that these might make something new. That, after all, was why I was in Lakeland at all, to find a new way of seeing and writing about this most "seen" and written about of landscapes.

But why seek such an elusive fluke of happenstance on High Rigg of all places – unsung High Rigg, among so many more celebrated Lakeland set pieces that I must try and get used to calling "fells"? It is a good question. I needed a viewpoint that knows the Lakes from the outside edge looking in, for was that not exactly what I was attempting myself? And a viewpoint that has something of all the elements of Lakeland within itself, a self-contained Lakeland miniature but with wide sightlines to some of the famed set-pieces of England's landscape superstars. In that regard at least, I was well qualified, for I have made something of a study of such eminences in my native land: small mountains that reveal the character of whole mountain ranges in ways that are hidden when you are in among those greater landscapes, simply because of their aloof stance. Besides, I live on the edge of a mountain land that is something of a northern kinsman to this Lakeland corner – the eastern half of the Loch Lomond and the Trossachs National Park, the Highland part of Stirling. So I know the mountains, glens, rivers, burns, lochs, wetlands, woods and wildness of the land I call the Highland Edge among the first mountains of the Highlands, 200 miles to the north of High Rigg, and whence for the last forty-something years my instincts have been inclined to venture west and further north, and sometimes back east to my native shore around the Firth of Tay. But south? Hardly ever. My brother, Vic, lived in Lancaster for many years and we had walked often enough in Lakeland, but mostly in the southern fells and not in any purposeful fashion. So what was I doing on High Rigg, tentatively trying to pin down the names of summits from the unfamiliar map and compass in my hands?

It had begun with a visit to Ullswater. I warmed to an unexpected familiarity that stemmed from the way it lies in the Lakeland landscape as a slender curve, with one end almost in the lowlands and the other immersed deep in a cluster of mountains. Back where I have plied much of my nature writer's trade, along that southern edge of the Highlands of Scotland, I have fashioned a notional "nature writer's territory" where much of my day-to-day, sea-son-by-season, year-on-year fieldwork happens. At its heart is a loch that lies in its landscape as a slender curve with one end almost in the lowlands and the other immersed deep in a cluster of mountains. Its name is Loch Lubnaig, and Ullswater is its Sasunnach kin, its sister-in-landscape. I happened to mention my visit in an email to my publisher, Sara Hunt, who is herself a native of this "The North" that lies so far in my south. Her response was not quite what I expected: might I like to write something set in Lakeland, where a mountain is a fell, a burn is a beck, a lochan is a tarn and – crucially – a loch is a lake? Would I like to write about Lakeland? I suppressed a creeping ambivalence while I assessed what I was up against, and weighed all that against the undeniable fact that Sara has very good instincts about such things. A timely book festival event in Carlisle was also an opportunity to spend a spare hour in a good independent bookshop called Book Case, and which has a Cumbria and Scotland Room. I never did get round to seeing what the Scotland section had to offer, because the Cumbria section was on the teeming side of what you might call comprehensive. If there was a gap in the market, I wasn't seeing it. Unless…unless two spores adrift on contrary winds should chance to coincide and their fusion give birth to a different species of Lakeland book, a book like this one.

So some little time later I was on the road south again to "The North". I had put the M80, the M73, the M74, the M6 and a few westbound miles of the A66 behind me, and with a truly startling suddenness, there lay a breathless tranquillity where a good-natured, sweet-watered burn shone in the sun, and I told myself at once that I must learn to call it a beck. I had studied my troublingly new map and I was on my way to High Rigg. And the land seemed to reach out a hand and bid me welcome to St John's in the Vale and the start of something new.

That view and its singularly un-Scottish name produced an instant response: "That could not be a Scottish valley, could it?" It was a simple assessment of a species of beauty that was unfamiliar to me, and its difference reassured me even before I had troubled to try and pin down what it was about the valley that was different. And then, beyond St John's in the Vale, looking across to what I now know to be Clough End and the Dodds (Great Dodd, Watson's Dodd, Stybarrow Dodd… *a land not named by my native tongue, the words are awkward*) a rainbow sprung into brilliant life, and the welcome seemed complete.

Ah yes, the rainbow. Omens. Peregrine, rainbow, shallow curves of flight and light, one of no colour at all and one of all the colours, yet as complementary as held hands. Does falcon see rainbow for what it is, and why it flares and fades? Does its bird brain grasp the essential principle of physics that go to work to make a rainbow? Yes, but it has different words for it: that's my guess. But now I am running ahead of myself.

There was, first of all, the church. I didn't come here to write about churches, at least not unless they honour nature, contribute to the landscape in some way: say, an owl nest in a belfry, or a particularly elegant, organic stance on the rock of the land, as if the God it serves had commanded it to stand there, and only there, and become landscape. Alas, the church in question was rather a darkly prosaic huddle of stones hard under the north-facing prow of High Rigg, with the dimensions and architectural cut of a Victorian peasant cottage and a bell-tower and a porch so out of proportion that all they added was ungainliness. The north of England is well populated with bonny kirks that serve their landscapes well. This is not one of these. And yet, that good-natured, sweet-watered beck down there is named for it: St John's Beck. And that valley, the one that could not be Scottish, is St John's in the Vale, and there was no denying that I would want to engage with such a landscape within these first few introductory hours. So I spared the church a second glance. The surprise is inside: the altar is gorgeous, with hints from the 1860s of the arts and crafts movement to come. Surely whoever designed that particular silk purse was not responsible for the sow's ear of the church? No architect lays claim to the church of 1848 (and why would they?), but the altar (removed from another church near Keswick twenty years later) was the work of George Gilbert Scott. Enter the third omen. Arguably the most handsome building in my hometown of Dundee is the museum and art gallery, the McManus. It is the work of George Gilbert Scott. So I am not the first to plough this furrow between the valleys of the River Tay and St John's Beck and to give that unlovely kirk a second glance, and that too was an omen that reassured.

And this is a north-tending land. The plug formed by High Rigg and Low Rigg (its joined-at-the-hip twin to the north) resisted the sculpting tug of a glacier, but now post-glacial Lakeland asks nothing more demanding of it than to thrust apart the valley's two gentle waters, so now St John's Beck to the east and Naddle Beck to the west are perpetual neighbours and strangers. If their waters commingle at all, it will happen in the west-making River Greta, into which they both flow but half a mile apart. In turn, the Greta defers at Keswick to the River Derwent, which flows north into Bassenthwaite Lake's south-east corner, and out again by its north-west corner whence it flows west to the sea at Cockermouth. It was there, more than 200 years ago, that the Derwent was immortalised as *a voice that flowed along my dreams*, which students and admirers of William Wordsworth will recognise as one of the opening lines of the blank-verse autobiography-in-nature that the world has since come to know as "The Prelude". I wrote this in the month of the 250th anniversary of Wordsworth's birth (and the 170th of his death). The fusion of poet and landscape is more lauded than ever, two more spores that between them made something new: the Lakeland that Wordsworth wrote down was like no one else's, and that is still the case today. If you ever wondered what immortality looks like, it looks like Wordsworth's take on Lakeland.

Meanwhile, these two becks that flowed along my own daydreams either side of High Rigg were whispering, muttering syllables of that same voice Wordsworth heard, nothing less than the last living kin of the valley's glacier. A lane curved west from the church of St John's in the Vale and between High Rigg and Low Rigg, then south above Naddle Beck until its path was crossed by a drystone wall. To follow the lane felt like keeping the Lakeland I sought at arm's length, the gentlest of tiptoeing preliminaries. It took a few moments before I understood that the wall was my way in. It took the slope at a gentle angle and a little above waist-height, rose and curved across and between contrary and complementary slopes, a path that rode the contours with the ease and style of a file of red deer, and so hand-in-glove with nature that it looked at once as if any other line would have seemed forced and unnatural. So sure was the eye, so accomplished the skill of the builder-of-walls that he first envisioned a work that would bind the landscape in a benevolent clasp, then stone-on-stone he gave physical, three-dimensional truth to his vision. So he built a beautiful wall which set down where he knew that, rather than intrude, rather than impose on the landscape, it would embellish and enhance. In time, the art of the builder-of-walls would become landscape itself.

Built stone as landscape: I had never been struck by the idea before. But when it is this good, when it is fashioned from the raw stuff of the hillside, when it lies across the face of the land in such a way that when you think of that little corner of Lakeland you remember the hills and the way they fell towards each other *and* you remember the wall the way you might remember something the glacier left behind. There is no higher compliment.

And you remember the tree. The wall might have been laid that way to draw your eye to the tree, although there are chicken-and-egg connotations to the question of which came first. The tree stands at the very point in the landscape where the wall disappears from view and it is quite alone. It is tall and elegant, fully grown, and because I met it on an autumn-into-winter kind of day it was quite bare, which is the way I like a big deciduous tree best because it reveals its true shape, and this one forked low down, but then it reached tall with all its limbs but one, and stayed slender. In its between-the-seasons clothes, it rose out of a hillside clad in wintry bracken, which is the best kind if you must have bracken, for it had shrunk to knee-high and wore an agreeable shade of muted tawny fire.

So I climbed by the wall, pleased with its company, and at the tree I turned left and north onto High Rigg's main south ridge, and at once the land started to open. I said a silent thank you to the builder-of-walls, another to the maker-of-small-mountains, and a third to the benevolent guiding spirit that had urged me to start with High Rigg.

★ ★ ★

The ridge of High Rigg is hollowed and humped with tiny tarns littered with tinier grassy islands, as if the Great Ice that shaped this place had toyed with a maquette of all Lakeland before it determined the final design, and this was it. The summit that late November day was wind-tormented. The day was sunny-squally, and there is nothing better than sunny-squally for fast weather, a mobile sky and rainbows. So having slaked a mountain thirst on the north-ward prospects to Blencathra and Skiddaw, a curtain wall fashioned from Skiddaw slate sprawled across the north of "The North" and probably designed by geology to hold back the pesky Scots, and having benefitted from a master-class in mountain identification through 360 degrees, I turned again to the near distance and my eye lit on St John's in the Vale (the valley, not the church), and I saw its myriad small enclosed fields, enclosed in stone walls and, as often as not, lines of trees, saw how the low ground was broad and flat and well worked, and how the hills rose sharply from the very edges of the well-worked land, and it so refreshed my unaccustomed gaze that I thought:

"That could not be a Scottish valley."

As if to disprove that less than riveting deduction, a squall fashioned in Scotland thrashed south and straight across the rock where I stood, and at once the sun blazed behind it and when I turned back to the valley that wasn't Scottish, it was to find it linked to its mountain by a rainbow fit for the gods.

Then the peregrine.

It had been there in the corner of my eye when I turned to utter my self-evident truth about the valley that could not be Scottish and then the squall struck and then the rainbow, and these in tandem conspired to make me turn away, but the peregrine flew into the rainbow as if it might burst the arch asunder and splinter its spectrum into shimmering shards of red, orange, yellow, green, blue, indigo and violet. But rainbows are immune to peregrines and (it seemed to me) the peregrine rose and fell in shallow glides on the air in mimicry of the rainbow arch. And then it fell away and became missile and somewhere down there in St John's in the Vale was the object of its endgame, and the rainbow faded and a fast raincloud skipped through the valley and briefly obliterated the green and stone-patterned fields, and just for a few seconds, a very few seconds, it could just have been a Scottish valley.

Omens. Sometimes they astound me. Sometimes they just catch in my throat. But suddenly, this little nowhere under the rainbow felt like the perfect place to begin.

Two

The Tree Mountaineers (I)

But worthier still of note
Are those fraternal four of Borrowdale,
Joined in one solemn and capacious grove;
Huge trunks! And each particular trunk a growth
Of intertwisted fibres serpentine
Up-coiling, and inveterately convolved;
Nor uninformed with fantasy, and looks
That threaten the profane…
…beneath whose sable roof
Of boughs as if for festal purpose, decked
With unrejoicing berries, ghostly shapes
May meet…

> – from "Lorton Vale Yew Trees", by William Wordsworth

HAVE YOU EVER SEEN a great grey owl, the once-seen-never-forgotten spectre of boreal forest, the phantom of the north and the ghost of the forest in various folklores scattered across the far north of the northern hemisphere? It is a sizeable phantom: a yard tall and a five-foot wingspan, but it weighs not much more than two pounds so that when it flies it floats, and its prey never knows it's there until a shadow the size of a raincloud darkens the last moments of vole, gopher, rat, mouse, grouse. They have a trait they share with wolves: the capacity to stop dead and vanish where they stand. When they perch next to a tree trunk, or settle into a nest in the fork of a tree robust enough to accommodate the bulk of a pair of them, then they simply become tree trunk. So why, given that the range of the great grey owl is North America, Scandinavia and northern Russia, and the nearest one to Borrowdale (a little to the south of Derwentwater) is likely to be in Norway (a little to the north of the Arctic Circle), why am I asking if you have ever seen one?

On the Ordnance Survey map for West Cumbria, two words: *Borrowdale Yews*. Now why would the Ordnance Survey mention yew trees on a map? My instincts twitched. I like yew trees. The most famous yew tree of them all, at Fortingall in Perthshire, is no more than an hour's drive from my home. It may be the oldest living organism in Europe, anything between 4,000 and 9,000 years old. No one knows, and unless someone devises a method of determining the age of trees that does not involve counting annular rings, no one ever will know. But the Fortingall Yew and I are practically on first-name terms.

Yew trees decompose from the inside out. They grow old by munching their own innards, scoffing their own annular rings. After 2,000 years they may have achieved a still-vertical trunk of improbable girth but which is little more than a timber membrane a few inches thick enclosing nothing; a husk but a vigorous husk, a living hollow, a ghost tree. Old yew trees are not pretty, not photogenic, they don't make good postcards or good art, but they are among nature's miracles. So when the map in my hands singled out their presence for special mention *−Borrowdale Yews*, as if it was its own place − it caught my attention.

Yet if you were to lift your eyes from the crammed whorls of contour lines onto which the words *Borrowdale Yews* have been printed in the map's smallest typeface, making them all but unreadable, then look across to where the contour lines translate into living hillside − the lowest slopes of Seatoller Fell on the far side of the River Derwent's upper reaches − and if you had never seen the Borrowdale Yews before or even heard of them (I hadn't); and if you were anticipating perhaps a yew wood or a yew plantation or even a yew copse (I was, otherwise why put them on a map?)...in that case, it is quite possible that your heart would sink (mine did) at the first sight of an apparently mangy green blot on the otherwise fair face of their hillside. It is equally possible that the heart-sinking would be followed by an anguished groan:

"Is that it? Is that all there is?"

I admit to uttering just such a groan. But I had come this far, and I told myself that surely there had to be a reason why these particular yews had caught the eye of the Ordnance Survey. No sooner had that unreliable thought emerged through the disappointment than I imagined the massed ranks of seasoned veterans of these hills and many more besides, not to mention the hobnailed ghosts of their long-departed predecessors, all sadly shaking their heads and with one voice muttering into their beer:

"Not necessarily."

In any case, it was but a short upstream walk to a bridge across the Derwent, a slightly longer one on the far side back downstream to the unenthralling smudge of the trees. Besides, the act of crossing the bridge unveiled a lowering sorcerer-sun's endeavours to lengthen and realign the shadows among the mountains that cradle the Derwent's headwaters: Great Gable, and a north-making thrust of Scafell Pike (Round How and Great End and Seathwaite Fell), and the curve of cliffs that cradles Angle Tarn under Bow Fell. The language of this landscape growls like landslides in my Scottish head, clattering its unaccustomed sounds all around the consciousness of one raised on the softer-tongued Gaelic vocabulary of *beinn* and *sgurr*, *creag* and *carn*, *gleann* and *lochan*. All this is going to take time and guidance. What matters is that I find a way to fit more seamlessly into the landscape itself than into its language. I can relish the differences in the landscape even as I try to reconcile the angular bluntness of that language to represent such beauty.

★ ★ ★

I turned north to follow the River Derwent downstream. The water had the clarity of mountain air. It coursed and chattered over soothingly curved boulders and lesser stones toned bluey-greeny-grey with the occasional startling intrusion of blood-red. So even if the Borrowdale Yews appeared at first glance and from a distance to lack panache, their neighbourhood river was unarguably beautiful, and this deep into the mountains it was both wild and demonstrably true to its distant glacial lineage. The yews, whatever their story, had rooted in a mountain landscape of some charm.

Suddenly the sun stepped free of some skyline mountain edge and fired up the autumn-shaded hillside. Bracken may be nature's pain-in-the-arse child, but it dies back (it "goes over", as they seem to say hereabouts) with agreeable burnish. Hugh MacDiarmid (I wonder if it might be judged a touch heretical to cite such a potent Lowland Scot in this land of wall-to-wall Wordsworth and Wainwright? Probably) wrote of such bracken beds in his poem "Bracken Hills in Autumn":

Their dense growth shuts the narrow ways
Between the hills and draws
Closer the wide valley's jaws

MacDiarmid had an unerring eye for landscape, and the sentiment fits Borrowdale's Lakeland fells as well as it fitted Biggar's Southern Uplands hills that gave it life. The sunlight's new reach flooded the land in a dance of slanting shaft and sprawling shadow that left nothing untransformed. The river was lit and glittered silver and gold and it lurked smoky blue in the shadows. And then the moment began to recommend itself to the yews.

These had advanced out of distance while I walked with my eyes elsewhere, and now all was not as it had seemed. They were gathered in a tight little fenced-off cluster; fenced off because, as the sage of English woodland Oliver Rackham once remarked, "In England, trees grow where people have not prevented them." Not a moment too soon, the Borrowdale Yews had been judged worth protecting from the people and their sheep-heavy, hill-farming tendencies. The 21st century has also afforded them a stile and a gratuitous information board, the gist of which is that Wordsworth was here (in 1826, since you asked, and he called the trees "the fraternal four" in what is, frankly, one of the lesser accomplishments of his oeuvre), that the fraternal four are now the fraternal three because of subsequent storm damage, and that it will be okay for you and me to cross the stile as long as we visit respectfully and don't inflict further suffering on the fraternal three. I'm paraphrasing.

The trees, it transpired, were extraordinary. Bruised and broken and bloodied, wounded and gouged and misshapen, but extraordinary nevertheless. If you like trees that have been redesigned and redefined several times by great age, and aren't done with the redesigning and the redefining yet, the Borrowdale Yews represent a vigorous and creative response to the last 2,000 years, give or take a few hundred years either side. They impose their atmosphere on you, an atmosphere that contrives to constrain how you behave in their company, so that your pace slows and softens. Don't be surprised if you feel the overwhelming urge to bow at certain moments in certain places, or to talk to them very, very quietly. Even at such close quarters, ancient yew trees are not pretty. Yet there is a species of beauty lurking amid the worry lines and decrepitude inflicted by the burden of standing still for 2,000 years of mountain weather, and, once you have got your eye in, that beauty will astound you, the closer you approach the more astounding. There is no noble profile of trunk and limbs, no spreadeagled canopy, for such age corrupts their capacity to behave like other trees. Foliage droops, yet when it reaches the ground – and it will – it digs in and roots again, a process that hints at the very real possibility of immortality. Limbs sag and succumb to storm or just the deadweight of their own living selves, then give up the unequal struggle and break off. And the trunks are shape-shifters. Not only will they confound every idea you ever entertained about what a tree might look like (in Fortingall, the ultimate girth the yew achieved is marked out in the ground by a circle of pegs, the diameter of which is sixty-five feet), not only pull themselves apart and peel themselves back to reveal the nothingness within, but in the process they also create one of nature's unique art forms.

The first manifestation of the phenomenon that I met at Borrowdale, head-on and without warning, was a great grey owl, or something very like it. So, to return to my initial question, if you have never seen a great grey owl, never seen it stand on a tree stump and make that stump look a yard taller than it actually is – for the owl has become stump, and the stump has become owl – never seen its wingspan open and darken the forest floor beneath, or seen it perched looking troublingly larger than life-size against the trunk of one of the Borrowdale Yews, you may find yourself wondering (with a certain amount of incredulity) what it's doing here.

True to the reputation of folklore, it is a ghost-owl, a forest phantom. This, it seems, is a landscape well populated with various tribes of ghosts, which rather endears it to me. The ghost-owl is a recurring motif in the accidental art that flourishes in the millennia-long sprawl of the life of a truly old yew tree. I was looking all around me from the heart of this extraordinary, compact woodland relic with its atmosphere and scent of great age and great decay, then I turned again and there it was, a great grey owl at twenty paces. It stared at me with jet-black eye sockets, its great round head was only partially obscured by wisps of frayed yew fronds, torn shards of limp foliage. Its lower legs and talons were clamped to the swollen mass of roots. These created the troublesome illusion of an owl with half a dozen legs (pity the short-tailed field vole that chances that way and looks up), and these the tree thrust outwards and downwards to overcome the obstacle presented by a substantial rock. At first glance, the whole was an eccentric extrusion on the unpretty flank of the trunk's shapelessness. But it became something "other" in my mind when I felt its eyes holding my gaze, following my careful movements, scrutinising my stillness.

In that moment I became a student of yew tree art, and that was how, over a meticulous exploration of the fraternal three's enclosure, I also found a barn owl, an eagle head with mouth open to reveal a pink sliver of tongue, two elvers swimming in a rushing torrent and, even more surprisingly, two cartoon-like sketches for Munch's "The Scream", side by side on the same trunk, as if the artist had decided to give himself a choice of approaches.

The barn owl was winking. Either that or it had lost its right eye, but I am going with winking because I know from personal experience that, sometimes, real barn owls do just that, so why shouldn't a ghost barn owl? It was a huge close-up of the two eyes and the top of the beak, but, crucially in the interests of creating the barn owl illusion, the yew in question had shed its bark, and over the bark-less decades (centuries?) the wood had mellowed to a perfect blend of barn owl shades, honeyed to a subtlety even the most fastidious artist could never hope to achieve. One eye – the wide-open one – was deep dark brown, almost black, with two pinpricks of white light. It looked like a troublingly intact and glossy eye from a distance, but in reality and at close quarters, it was a hole revealing the tree's darkly hollow interior. Immediately to the eye's left the tree thrust out a slim, curved wedge of those off-white and honey shades to make a more-than-passable suggestion of the beak. Beyond that was the second eye, a depression in the surface of the wood, which, more than anything else you could ever imagine, was a perfect stand-in for a closed barn owl eye.

Behold the winking owl.

To find a barn owl fashioned by nature's hand from still-living yew wood in this new-to-me landscape was one more good omen, for barn owls have been central to my life since childhood. Barn owls made a warrior for nature out of me, aged about seven or eight. I have told that particular story in a small book (mysteriously titled *Barn Owl*) that is one of a series of short monographs collectively titled *Encounters in the Wild*, and which I have been writing at irregular intervals since 2014. I think of the barn owl as an ambassador of life on the edge, a haunter of dawns and dusks, the restless sentry of the outside edge of the woods, with one eye on the grassy banks and one on the first and last tree shadows. The edge of things has long been my pre-ferred terrain as a nature writer: the edge of the land, the edge of the sea, islands beyond the edge of the land; the edge of the Highlands, where it collides with the edge of the Lowlands and where the wildlife tribes of both realms overlap. Now, with this invitation to write about Lakeland, I have adhered to instinctive preference and settled on its north-eastern edge, a landscape set off by the proximity of comparatively low-lying, river-strewn lands. It is the relict wildness of Lakeland I have set myself to uncover, not its famous ridges and summits, nor the tourist-drenched innards, for I like my mountains much quieter than these, and I am content to have them there in the exquisite middle-distance whenever I raise my head from bird or fox or flower or the disconcerting stare of a great grey owl at twenty paces. If I had qualms (it is undeniable, that fish-out-of-water sensibility) about taking on the project, I derived yet more reassurance from a barn owl carved into the trunk of what could well be a 2,000-year-old yew tree, carved by nature itself, and I found it every bit as life-affirming as the rainbow, the living peregrine.

And there were those other motifs that kept on emerging under scrutiny of one yew trunk or another. The most vivid, because it suggested ecstatic motion, was the pair of elvers, each a few inches long with dark heads and slender, sinuous bodies, "swimming" parallel courses through a rushing watercourse. They were heads-down and vertical when I found them, but the sense of moving water and swimming was enhanced by turning a digital photograph on its side, so that the vertical cracks and ridges and valleys of the bark and barkless patches appeared to flow horizontally, and so did the elvers. But had it not been for the huge, obvious presence of the great grey owl, I might never have found the elvers and the barn owl and the eagle. And I am still pondering the significance in such company of the two takes on "The Scream", the two heads almost touching, and each of them has two eyes and an open mouth and domed forehead, but no raised hands.

★ ★ ★

Two words on the map. *Borrowdale Yews.* Three trees inside a fence, but trees such as you may never have seen in your life. Trees inhabited by creatures of their own devising, as if they had given birth to them. Trees that have ridden the restless surf and storm of millennia with bravado and grace. Trees possessed of that quality which, in a human being, we would call "character". The American writer John Hay suggested of trees in his book *In Defense of Nature* (Viking Press, 1970):

> *Their connections with animate and inanimate things might just as well be called personal.*

His compatriot Fred Hagender wrote in *The Spirit of Trees (Floris Books, 2000):*

> *A yew that appears to be a hollow, decaying wreck is often at the beginning of its self-generation process. Yew can resurrect itself from complete decay. There is no biological reason for a yew tree to die – it can virtually live forever.*

And John Muir attributed something similar to the Sierra juniper in *My First Summer in the Sierra*:

Surely the most enduring of all tree mountaineers, it never seems to die a natural death, or even to fall after it has been killed. If protected from accidents, it would perhaps be immortal.

And what was William Wordsworth getting at when he wrote these lines in "Lorton Vale Yew Trees"?

Move along these shades
In gentleness of heart, with gentle hand
Touch – for there is a spirit in the woods.

I am not sure, but the sentiment reminds me of a conversation I had on one of many visits to the Fortingall Yew in Perthshire. If you don't know it, it is dingily imprisoned behind a combination of a high stone wall and high iron railings and a padlocked iron gate (I have long had a mind to borrow a JCB, obliterate the wall and railings and liberate the yew and let it take its chances in the wildwood again, not least because I think perhaps Fred Hagender is right). On this occasion, I had watched a group of loud, chattering visitors reading the copious information panels as they approached from their coach by the tourist industry's approved walk-this-way footpath. One woman detached herself from the group, skipped the tourist industry's official preamble, and came to stand nearby. She fretted by the bars. A camera was in her hand. I sympathised:

"It's not easy to photograph, is it?"

But I had misread her mood.

"Oh I don't care about that," she said. "I'd just like to touch it."

With Wordsworth's "gentle hand", I guessed from her demeanour. And perhaps she knew about the spirit in the woods too.

All of that was years before I had cause to pore over a map of West Cumbria, before I had stumbled across two words where the upper reaches of the River Derwent flow through Borrowdale. Before I saw the words *Borrowdale Yews* and thought, why mention yews on a map?

Three

Nature's Social Union

Now that I have invoked William Wordsworth and John Muir in the same breath, it is worth pausing to consider an observation expressed by Jonathan Bate in his biography, *Radical Wordsworth* (Collins, 2020):

> *As Muir was essential to the movement to preserve the "wilderness" of the American west, so Wordsworth was essential to the mind and writing of Muir.*

A moment of honesty is required here. I am a long-standing admirer and student of John Muir's writing; Wordsworth, less admired and less studied. So if what Mr Bate writes is true, then consider this. Can Wordsworth lay claim to sowing the original seed that rooted in a series of great minds and finally flowered in Muir's to give the world the concept of national parks? Are national parks Wordsworth's invention, rather than Muir's? Apart from anything else, it is quite a thought to intrude on the ruminations of a 21st-century Scot as his own mind was being gently blown by the quiet wonders of what is left of the Borrowdale Yews. I had always thought that it was Robert Burns who turned Muir's head towards a deeper appreciation of nature, and for that matter, that he also turned the head of the young Wordsworth, and for that matter the maturing Wordsworth. By the time Wordsworth published his first edition of *Lyrical Ballads* and began working on "The Prelude" (the same year – 1798), Burns's song was already sung. He had died two years earlier. And eleven years before that, he wrote what was surely the first poetic utterance of what we now know as nature conservation, in a poem which has since travelled the world. To give it its full title, "To A Mouse, on Turning Up Her Nest With the Plough, November 1785" is that rarest of literary phenomena: the perfect poem. For the purposes of my argument, however, consider the second verse, in which Burns slips out of his native Lowland Scots tongue for a moment to deliver this, in English:

I'm truly sorry man's dominion
Has broken nature's social union,
And justifies that ill opinion
Which makes thee startle
At me, thy poor earth-born companion,
And fellow mortal!

I am forever holding this verse up for Scots and non-Scots alike to contemplate and admire. It is remarkable for three reasons. Firstly, the apology is not just the lowly ploughman's to the lowly mouse, its subtext is all human-kind to all nature. Burns was aware that his own species had betrayed its place in nature's scheme of things, and was in the throes of destroying nature, bit by bit. The plough's desecration of the winter nest of a harvest mouse was a small symptom of that infinitely greater ill. Secondly, he does not distinguish between the status of man and mouse. They are earth-born companions and fellow mortals. Elsewhere in Burns's poetry he is fiercely critical of shooting and human indifference to the fate of wild creatures.

And thirdly, there is the use of an extraordinary phrase – "nature's social union". How did he come up with a concept like that? Any scrutiny of the few known influences on Burns as a poet reveal nothing at all. The conclusion I draw, with some confidence, is that the concept is a wholly original one. In our own century, we make free with the expression "the natural world", as if there is more than one world and the natural one is somewhere out there, just beyond the unnatural one we all inhabit. Burns knew better. His natural world was the one he lived in, the one he wrote about, the one that found his equal, his native kin, in a harvest mouse, in nature's social union.

What does all this have to do with Lakeland? A least part of the answer is to be found by travelling from Burns's Ayrshire to the valley of the Wye, and forward in time from 1785 to 1798. If you read Wordsworth's "Lines Written a Few Miles above Tintern Abbey, on Revisiting the Banks of the Wye during a Tour, July 13, 1798", there is first the rambling similarity to the title of Burn's poem – event, circumstances, date – then consider these lines in which Wordsworth becomes aware of a "sense sublime" in the landscape:

Of something far more deeply interfused,
Whose dwelling is the light of the setting suns,
And the round ocean and living air,

And the blue sky, and in the mind of man –
A motion and a spirit that impels
All thinking things, all objects of all thought,
And rolls through all things.

Might not another of like mind, standing there beside him, also have identified that same "sense sublime" which "rolls through all things" and referred to it instead as "nature's social union"? The human race is but one of Earth's wonders; others include the moon and the other stars of a shared universe, the mountains, forests, becks, tarns, lakes, birds, beasts, flowers, insects and the harvest mouse's winter nest. Wordsworth knew and admired Burns's work, even name-checked him in *Lyrical Ballads* in the company of an invented pedlar:

…His eye
Flashing poetic fire, he would repeat
The songs of Burns, and as we trudged along
Together did we make the hollow grove
Ring with our transports. Though he was untaught,
In the dead lore of schools undisciplined,
Why should he grieve? He was a chosen son:
To him was given an ear which deeply felt
The voice of Nature in the obscure wind
The sounding mountain and the running stream.
To every natural form, rock, fruit and flower,
Even the loose stones that cover the highway
He gave a moral life; he saw them feel
Or linked them to some feeling. In all shapes

He found a secret and mysterious soul,
A fragrance and a spirit of strange meaning.

Behold Wordsworth in poetic genius mode, picking up the idea of nature's social union and running with it. And isn't it beautiful, and isn't it glorious? And isn't it also true?

The great good fortune that attended Wordsworth's transformation of the literature of the land was that he was born and lived his life in the right place at the right time. When the Lake District became one of Britain's first national parks in 1951, the wheel that finally came full circle was Wordsworth's wheel. Burns may have been the spark, but Wordsworth was what that spark lit up. Burns's poetry would travel the world, too, but on a different mission, as a champion of the rights of man – and woman: his "Green Grows the Rashes O" is still the only world-famous song that suggests God is female. But Wordsworth's poetry, and to a lesser extent the whole English Romanticism movement, produced shock waves in the New World, and it is there that his thinking found its true home, long before it bore fruit in the landscape that made him famous. So Wordsworth was in the right place because he made the Lakeland landscape leap from the page as a vision of nature's social union, and he was at the right time because…well, consider this particular chronology of overlapping lives:

Robert Burns, 1759–1796
William Wordsworth, 1770–1850
Ralph Waldo Emerson, 1803–1882
Henry David Thoreau, 1817–1862
Walt Whitman, 1819–1892

John Muir, 1836–1914

Aldo Leopold, 1887–1948

Emerson – essayist, philosopher, lecturer, poet and American – was the first to react. He wrote that Wordsworth had "no master but Nature and Solitude", and his admiration persuaded him to cross the Atlantic and visit Wordsworth in 1833. It seems he was disappointed in the man (by that time in his sixties and well past his creative prime), but inspired enough by his published genius to write the essay "Nature", which was published three years later. The introduction begins:

Nature is already, in its forms and tendencies, describing its own design. Let us interrogate the great apparition that shines so peacefully around us. Let us inquire, to what end is nature?

…Philosophically considered, the universe is composed of Nature and the Soul.

And then, in chapter one, there is this:

To go into solitude, a man needs to retire as much from his chamber as from society. I am not solitary whilst I read and write, though nobody is with me. But if a man would be alone, let him look at the stars…every night come out these envoys of beauty, and light the universe with their admonishing smile.

From such gentle beginnings, Emerson's essay took Wordsworth's radical ethos and gave it an American accent, after which attitudes to nature on both sides of the Atlantic would never be quite the same again. The essay considered eight different aspects of the relationship between nature and humankind. Its publication in 1836 was not a moment too soon for the stalled momentum of the revolution in the literature of the land that Wordsworth had initiated. Jonathan Bate listed in *Radical Wordsworth* the things about the poet's life he hoped to explain, including "why the poetry of the first half is so memorable, that of the second so forgettable." You could say that Emerson's "Nature" filled the vacuum. And in another way, the timing was perfect, for the stir it created was not lost on a young man who was then a senior student at Harvard. He read it, swallowed it whole, digested it, and found his life transformed, its direction determined. His name was Henry David Thoreau. You might say that Emerson's essay engendered in that young man *a secret and mysterious soul, / A fragrance and a spirit of strange meaning*; you might even say that directly because of it he became an ambassador for "nature's social union".

So Burns had fired Wordsworth, Wordsworth created something utterly new and fired Emerson, who fired Thoreau. Anyone else?

"I was simmering, simmering, simmering. Emerson brought me to a boil," wrote another poet who had created something new, a wholly American voice that would galvanise generations and goes on galvanising to this day. Walt Whitman. When no one knew quite what to make of his *Leaves of Grass,* he had sent it to Emerson, and back came the one endorsement he craved more than any other:

I am not blind to the worth of the wonderful gift of Leaves of Grass. I find it the most extraordinary piece of wit and wisdom that America has yet contributed...I give you joy for your free and brave thought. I have great joy in it. I find incomparable things said incomparably well, as they must be. I find the courage of treatment which so delights us, and which large perception only can inspire.

Emerson, Thoreau and Whitman were Wordsworth's American apostles. They spread the word along the eastern seaboard of the United States of America, and the word was transcendentalism. It invited its readers to consider that nature – not God – was the be all and end all, that everything in it had its own existence and (the word appears again and again in its copious literature, as stubbornly undefined as it was ubiquitous) its own soul. And, brother and sister, that includes you, for you too are nature. With Emerson, it was personal, for he had met Wordsworth and walked with him at his home in the epicentre of Lakeland, and that association between the genius and the landscape that nourished the literature and the philosophy that Emerson himself now espoused...that was a turning point in his life, and as it would turn out, a turning point in the relationship between people and landscape the world over. There is no doubt now that whatever the frailties in the 21st century's Lake District National Park – and there are many – the fact that it exists at all stemmed from that momentary meeting of minds at Rydal Mount. It had a long way to go from the shores of Rydal Water, both in terms of time and distance, but once it had crossed the Atlantic, then crossed America, galvanising the very concept of nature conservation, it returned and came home again. Without Emerson, would it ever have happened at all?

For Thoreau, it became a personal destiny, whose name was *Walden*. He and Emerson became lifelong friends, but it was trickier with Whitman. They mostly argued when they finally met, but in later years, Whitman had no doubts about Thoreau's worth. He wrote:

Thoreau was a surprising fellow — he is not easily grasped — is elusive, yet he is one of the native forces — stands for a fact, an upheaval...Thoreau was not so precious, tender, a personality as Emerson: but he was a force — he looms up bigger and bigger: his dying does not seem to have hurt him a bit...One thing about Thoreau keeps him very near to me: I refer to his lawlessness — his dissent — his going his own absolute road let hell blaze all it chooses.

The fact is that all three of the apostles, and especially Thoreau and Whitman, are alive and well in American culture in the 21st century, and many an American nature writer still reaches for them, still regards them as relevant, still admires and reveres. But the man who was to change everything for all of them, and for all America, and who would one day pay homage at Wordsworth's grave with a tear in his eye and a lump in his throat...he wasn't even born until two years after Emerson published "Nature", and on the far side of the Atlantic Ocean. In 1849, a man called Daniel Muir set sail for America accompanied by three of his six children. Among them was his eleven-year-old son,

John. The Scots were coming! They settled in Wisconsin, but as he grew up, young John was drawn more and more to the mountains of the west, and it was from there that in time, in time, he would change the world, and an idea that was first voiced in Lakeland by William Wordsworth made his dream a reality.

Is it possible that Muir simply heeded the advice of Thoreau, whose work he also admired ("...mankind progresses from east to west...we go westward into the future")? The Sierra Club's online John Muir Exhibit has this to say:

> The uniquely Transcendentalist School which formed in Harvard-influenced Cambridge brought a new idea regarding man, spirit and nature to a very young country struggling to find its voice. The young John Muir...took strongly to the Transcendentalist ideas at the University of Wisconsin. Much of his writing has a clear Emersonian ring...but his vision grew to be very unlike that of Emerson or any of the New England group...

The thought occurs: John Muir was not New England but New America. Emerson had finally found his man. The Sierra Club Exhibit goes on:

> ...For Muir, Transcendentalism was an experience of spirituality given meaning by direct physical immersion in nature – particularly her alpine areas...When they finally met in Yosemite in 1871, their pleasant meeting belied the differing forces which compelled their thoughts and actions. The young Muir could only conclude that Emerson's ideas of

nature began and ended in an abstract metaphysical realm which was frustratingly insufficient to satisfy Muir's spiritual yearnings...

Nevertheless, Emerson had helped to shape both his thinking and writing. Here is Emerson writing in "Nature" in 1836:

A leaf, a drop, a crystal, a moment of time, is related to the whole, and partakes of the perfection of the whole. Each particle is a microcosm and faithfully renders the likeness of the world.

And here, almost sixty years later, is Muir, adapting that idea into one of his endlessly quotable lines:

When we try to pick out anything by itself, we find it hitched to everything else in the universe.

Emerson would prove to be the foundation stone on which Muir went to work. When the Sierra Club exhibit made the point that "Muir not only observed nature, but physically immersed himself in it – a baptism so to speak..." the metaphor was Muir's own. It occurs in an essay titled "Twenty Hill Hollow":

Never shall I forget my baptism in this font. It happened in January...The Hollow overflowed with light, as a fountain, and only small, sunless nooks were kept for mosseries and ferneries. Hollow Creek spangled and mazed like a river. The ground steamed with fragrance. Light of unspeakable richness was brooding the flowers…The sunshine for a whole summer seemed condensed into the chambers of that one glowing day. Every trace of dimness had been washed from the sky; the mountains were dusted and wiped clean with clouds…the grand Sierra stood along the plain, coloured in four horizontal bands: – the lowest, rose purple; the next higher, dark purple; the next, blue; and above all, the white row of summits, pointing to the heavens.

It may be asked, What have mountains fifty or a hundred miles away to do with Twenty Hill Hollow? To lovers of the wild, these mountains are not a hundred miles away. Their spiritual power and the goodness of the sky make them near, as a circle of friends. They rise as a portion of the hilled walls of the Hollow. You cannot feel yourself out of doors; plain, sky, and mountains ray beauty which you feel. You bathe in these spirit-beams, turning round and round, as if warming at a camp-fire. Presently you lose consciousness of your own separate existence: you blend with the landscape, and become part and parcel of nature.

This wasn't so much radically new thinking as radically old. The language of the First Nation tribes of old America is alive with the sense of a way of life that honoured nature, that regarded themselves as but one more of nature's creatures; learning from the most influential of nature's non-human tribes techniques of hunting, survival and seasonal migration; fashioning and honouring their own sacred rites that deepened their spiritual connection with land, water, sky, bear, wolf, eagle, salmon, buffalo. They did not live in order to *become* part and parcel of nature, they lived *because* they were part and parcel of nature, and had been from the first. Unlike the white Europeans, they never saw any reason to be otherwise. But so overwhelming was the white man's impact on the land of America that even by Muir's time, he was an exception to the rule, a throwback.

But what made him truly different from all that had gone before him was that he apprehended the threats to all nature from his own species and became an activist for nature long before the word or the concept had been invented. There were no rule books, no literature, no protocols, no political processes to accommodate his activism, so he wrote his own. By his example and his eloquence, he won a hearing for nature and his powers of persuasion reached all the way to the President of the United States, and through his persuasion (notwithstanding that Wordsworth had hinted at the possibility in the English Lake District almost 100 years before) John Muir finally gave the world national parks. Muir was, literally and metaphorically, a force of nature. Once he got to California, he fashioned a life for himself that afforded limitless time in the wildest landscapes of western and northern America, and amassed such a store of first-hand experience that whenever he talked about it in public or wrote it down, he was irresistible.

No one found him more irresistible than a young forestry student who was destined to become no less immortal in the annals and the literature of nature conservation than Muir himself. For what it's worth, in my own estimation that young forestry student's single book is the finest work of nature writing anywhere, ever. He was also the one who brought the Wordsworth-Emerson-Whitman-Thoreau-Muir axis into my own lifetime. He died in 1948, the year after I was born, and the year before his book was published. He was Aldo Leopold. His book was *A Sand County Almanac*. It has never been out of print. A *New York Times* review said it was "full of beauty and vigor and bite", which is more or less perfect. It becomes more relevant with every passing year, like Muir, like Thoreau. Passing years are the structure that underpins an essay in *A Sand County Almanac*, called "Good Oak", in which Leopold and another saw through a lightning-struck oak on his Winconsin sandfarm, and as the two-handled saw cuts from bark towards core he traces America's history in the tree's annular rings, until the saw reaches the core and starts travelling forward through time again. It was not lost on him that Muir had spent his youth nearby, and Leopold paid him this tribute, as the saw bit into 1865:

In that year John Muir offered to buy from his brother, who then owned the home farm thirty miles east of my oak, a sanctuary for the wildflowers that had gladdened his youth. His brother declined to part with the land, but he could not suppress the idea: 1865 still stands in Wisconsin history as the birth year of mercy for things natural, wild, and free.

A Sand County Almanac endures, like *Walden*, but it takes the arguments much further. Leopold got the spirit of activism from Muir. Muir founded the Sierra Club as well as the national park movement; Leopold founded the Wilderness Society, and he was a United Nations ambassador for the environment when he was killed fighting a neighbour's house fire in 1948. And Leopold has one more trait in common with Muir, a gift for writing quotably. There are few corners of that sphere of nature writing that ascends to literature where the following words from Leopold's foreword to *A Sand County Almanac* are not uttered with reverence:

> *Conservation is getting nowhere because it is incompatible with our Abrahamic concept of land. We abuse land because we regard it as a commodity belonging to us. When we see land as a community to which we belong, we may begin to use it with love and respect. There is no other way for land to survive the impact of mechanized man, nor for us to reap from it the esthetic harvest it is capable, under science, of contributing to culture.*
>
> *That land is a community is the basic concept of ecology, but that land is to be loved and respected is an extension of ethics. That land yields a cultural harvest is a fact long known, but latterly often forgotten.*

Nobody I know who works within or simply believes in nature conservation in Scotland is unfamiliar with those words. We did, after all, invent the John Muir Trust. To this day, the American nature writing tradition crosses the Atlantic and finds an eager readership here: in no particular order (other than that in which they cluster along my bookshelves) there is Barry Lopez, Annie Dillard, Catherine Feher-Elston, Nancy Lord, Lynn Schooler, David Gessner, Henry Beston, Ernest Thompson Seton, David M. Carroll among many more, all of them acknowledging specifically or implicitly their debt to something remarkable that took root in the English Lake District, crossed the Atlantic with Emerson, and never looked back. To this day, it blazes new trails.

I have become an email friend of David M. Carroll, a New Hampshire wetland specialist. His lifelong love of wetlands, and turtles in particular, has metamorphosed from art college to art teacher to passionate wetland activist to a writer whose literary gifts are as profuse and vivid as the artwork that graces all his books. If you were a turtle, you would want David on your side. I have quoted his work several times in my own books, particularly *Nature's Architect* (Saraband, 2015), about the reintroduction of the beaver to Scotland. I turned to his writing again in the context of researching this chapter, and in search of a sense of connection, however tenuous, between that great, unbroken 200-and-something-year-old tradition and my own work. What I found was in a short autobiography called *Self-Portrait with Turtles* (Houghton Mifflin Company, 2004), the copy he sent me with its very personal inscription, which was connection enough for me.

In eleventh-grade English, we were handed a book I had never heard of: Henry David Thoreau's Walden. From the opening paragraph, I was transfixed. The very idea of this book – its reason for being, its empathy with nature and view of human society – electrified me.

Reading some paragraphs was like finding fragments of my own turtle world come to life between the covers of a book.

I could taste his descriptions of the pondside, the marshes and swamps, fields and woods, light and seasons, his world just enough apart from the world of man to be the realm of nature.

By the time I read "How many a man has dated a new era in his life from the reading of a book!" I knew I could date a new era in my life from the reading of Thoreau. It was new not in the sense of a departure in a previously unknown direction but in affirmation, broadened revelation, deepened resolve. I found myself, as one of my favorite quotes of Robert Frost went, "only more sure of all I thought was true"...

...I embraced this radical treatise, this manifesto grounded in wildness. Quotes from Walden began to pepper my speech...

But in my own devotion to becoming lost in and absorbed by my wild-as-possible surroundings, I was not prone to Thoreauvian philosophical musings. It seemed that he went looking for lofty thoughts where I went looking for turtles. I felt at home in his book in a way that was curiously akin to how I felt at home with the turtles.

In walking the long days' avenues of sunlight along watery ditches by the railroad tracks, wading among the blueberry mounds and shrub thickets of the red-maple swamp, crouching in giant reeds beside spotted-turtle channels just upstream from the pulse of the tides, I felt that I was living the kind of time that permeates Walden. To paraphrase its author, time was but the stream I went a-turtling in.

So what arguably began with a mouse in an Ayrshire field in 1785, crossed the border to the English Lake District, crossed the Atlantic, crossed America from coast to coast and back again, and found its way onto my bookshelves more than two centuries later as a personal gift from its author, and where it sits beside Emerson, Thoreau, Whitman, Muir and Leopold and a heathy gathering of American nature writers who are still alive and well, and where these rub shoulders with Seton Gordon and all his descendants of the Scottish nature writing tradition…all that has just crossed the border again with this Scottish nature writer who has drunk freely from both traditions and who is on a mission to unearth what might yet survive of the Lakeland landscape where so much began. And suddenly there were two words on a map, *Borrowdale Yews*, and suddenly there was Wordsworth embalmed in the trunk of a yew tree and looking for all the world like a great grey owl.

★ ★ ★

There is one voice missing. One further voice that should – inevitably, I suppose – be added to that illustrious, centuries-spanning roll-call. This voice:

In due course I came to live within sight of the hills and was well content. If I could not be climbing, I was happy to sit idly and dream of them, serenely. Then came a restlessness and the feeling that it was not enough to take their great gifts and do nothing in return. I must dedicate something of myself, the best part of me, to them. I started to write about them, and to draw pictures of them. Doing these things, I found they were still giving and I still receiving, for a great pleasure filled me when I was so engaged – I had found a new way of escape to them and from all else less worthwhile.

If you never read anything else about Lakeland, I would urge you to read "Some Personal Notes in Conclusion" at the end of the book called *A Pictorial Guide to the Lakeland Fells being an illustrated account of a study and exploration of the mountains in the English Lake District by A. Wainwright, Book One, The Eastern Fells.* The title may lack concision, but it sets the tone for all that follows through seven volumes, for detail is Wainwright's stock-in-trade. That and a deep and timeless respect for "Lakeland's mountains and trees and water". At times, when you read Wainwright (as opposed to simply consulting him for his preferred route because you are unable or can't be bothered to give the landscape the time he gave it), it's almost as if he's talking to himself. Which may, explain this:

…this book has been written carefully and with infinite patience, for my own pleasure and because it has seemed to bring the hills to my own fireside. If it has merit, it is because the hills have merit.

Four

The Tree Mountaineers (2)

YES, THESE LAKELAND HILLS have merit. They are singular in
their tightly corralled beauty. They cluster along the flanks
of narrow valleys, jostle for headroom around headwaters.
The shadows they throw are unpredictable, sometimes
they startle. Outwith high summer, sunlight mostly lies
aslant, fired from wedges of sky; thwarted by parallel ridges,
right-angled ridges, acute and obtuse ridges, blunted by
buttresses and skinnier ridges that turn out to be sidings,
roads to nowhere, except that sometimes a terminal flourish leans far out and high above a valley you thought you
knew and startles with a new perspective, a new light, casts
a new shadow, a new spell. And this never ends, this sorcery
of light and dark. There is no end to Lakeland's spell. There
is no limit to the hills' merit.

Better-late-than-never winter dropped by in mid-Jan-
uary, wrapped a cold fur of frozen snow around the high
slopes, smothered the north-eastern corner of all Lakeland,
but wherever a valley bit westward into the massif, its northern flank was all but snowless and deep-shadowed, yet it
faced across that valley to an eye-narrowing blaze of white.
The snowless flank of one such valley was surely the most
uncharacteristically bland mountainside in the whole mer-
it-strewn Lakeland conglomeration. If you gave it a second
glance at all, you would see a steep, scree-and-heather-clad,
bluntly curved slump, a mountainous shrug. Snow lay along

its ridge but nowhere else. Yet over there, beyond the curve, beyond the slump, beyond the all-but-snowlessness, and unseen, unguessed-at from here, there was a hole in the mountain where the breath of an Arctic-born wind had been at work. In two days, this ice-dragon had transformed a high-walled coliseum with thick-crusted snow cliffs and floored it with a sheet of blue-grey ice called Bowscale Tarn. Apart from the outflow, where a barely melted beck you could step over muttered and squirted blackly beneath fat spheres of moulded ice that clung to inches-high banks of overhanging snow, all was still and silent as Lapland. You half expected reindeer, an Arctic fox.

In midday sunlight, aslant as ever, golden beams in parallel pairs so bright you could hardly bear to look at them, were teamed with pairs the same smoky shade as the tarn. Wild light, daring and unforgettable, fashioned a scaffolding of those beams and jammed it between corrie rim and corrie floor and galvanised a third of that crescent-curve of Lakeland rock with irresistible vitality. But elsewhere, in a gargantuan antidote, the headwall shivered in ghostly blues. The corrie only opens to the north. The ice-breathing dragon had charged in the front door, put in a few furious laps and gone straight out through the roof. Echoes of its stormy intrusion could still be seen in the sky. The wind stood on end in white clouds that rose from the rim in graceful curves, but these shredded as they climbed towards the blue of the upper sky. There were half a dozen such clouds, each one separated from its neighbour on either side by a matching curve of blue. It was that pattern that permitted the sunbeams to slice through to the wall and the floor. I can only imagine that this was the land dictating to the wind how it must behave as it crossed the mountains and their steep, sudden and narrow valleys, ridge after ridge. I further imagine the effect was to supercharge the wind. Such a challenge is not just why mountain winds are born, it's also why they travel a thousand miles south-west to indulge themselves in the landscape of Lakeland. Oh yes, these hills have merit. Even the Arctic winds know it.

But so fickle has winter become in the 21st century, even in the mountains of this land, that within days the tarn and its circle of cliffs looked weary, grey and pale, drained of energy and light. Snow and ice were reduced to pockmarks. The wind was back in its familiar south-westerly groove, so that if it promised weather at all, it promised rain. It was altogether too warm for ice dragons, and for that matter, for reindeer and Arctic foxes.

Following the beck upstream into the hills from the mountain village of Mungrisdale, the only shade in the landscape that wasn't grey or brown or wan green was the bright white of the throaty water invigorated by snowmelt. I was on a mission whose seeds had been sown a dozen miles to the south-west on the edge of the Derwent Fells above Buttermere: the Newlands Valley at the sopping end of a rain-bedevilled Lakeland day was clothed in the quiet light of a November afternoon. The land creaked under the weight of too much water. At its head, the waterfall of Moss Force raised its voice to an unflinching roar and commanded every passing eye to stand and stare. The pool at the foot of the highest of its three drops is garlanded by a small clutch of rowan trees. Quite apart from their essentially inhospitable stance, rooted as much in rock as in soil, they have days like this to contend with, days in which they are not only wind-thrashed and rain-lashed, but drenched from above and below by the fall.

The rowan is a tree mountaineer for the connoisseur. In Scotland – and doubtless in Lakeland's not so distant past – it is the golden eagle's tree of choice to freshen the eyrie cup with a stolen sprig of leaves. The great Scottish nature writer Seton Gordon cited two impressive examples of just what the species is capable of withstanding in his classic work, *The Cairngorm Hills of Scotland* (Cassell, 1925). One of these, at almost 2,000 feet in Glen Derry, was growing from an oak stump just tall enough to keep it of reach of deer, and which "thrust its main root down through the air and into level ground below. It had thus two root systems, one of them several feet below the other." Of the second tree, near Loch Coire an Lochan on Braigh Riabhach (Scotland's highest loch at 3,300 feet), Seton Gordon wrote:

It is a small and stunted rowan or mountain ash, sadly eaten by deer and perhaps by blue hares also. The small tree stands just over 3,000 feet above sea level. When it is remembered that a tree, even at 2,000 feet, is a rare thing in Scotland, it will be realised how exceptional is the altitude of this solitary rowan…

Given such a pedigree, the rowans of Moss Force have a lot to live up to, but live up to it they do, and those of us who stand and stare there on such a day of water on the move marvel anew every time. Samuel Taylor Coleridge famously waited deliberately for just such a day to clamber up by the banks of the fall, and, if the letter he wrote to Wordsworth's sister-in-law Sara Hutchinson is anything to go by, rather lost his marbles in the face of such a gesture of nature:

What a sight it is to look down on such a cataract…it is an awful image and Shadow of God and the World.

He explained to the long-suffering Sara his reasons for choosing such a day:

I have always found this stretched and anxious state of mind favourable to depth of pleasurable impression…The thing repaid me amply…

Hence an account in which he added to the English language's substantial vocabulary with inventions like "outjutment", "overbrows" and "circumvolve". His opiate tendencies are well enough known, but what on earth was he on when he saw Moss Force?

Great masses of water, one after the other, that in the twilight one might have feelingly compared them to a vast crowd of huge white bears, rushing one over the other, against the wind – their long white hair shattering abroad in the wind.

It was twilight when I left the rowans by their pool, but of the vast crowd of huge white bears there was neither hide nor long white hair. The Poetry Foundation explains how Coleridge learned the principles of composition and acquired his literary values at Christ's Hospital grammar school in London under the inspirational influence of the Reverend James Bowyer, and where "literary embroidery was discouraged". Where did it all go wrong, Sammy? Still, the thing repaid me amply too.

★ ★ ★

All rains stop falling eventually, even in Lakeland, and dusk in the Newlands Valley had a tawny cast. The land was rust-coloured, a sighing landscape in the aftermath of onslaught. A pale, thinly veiled half-moon was the brightest thing to cross that day's sky. The valley is backwater Lakeland, and all the better for that, and host to Keskadale Farm. The farm, in turn, is host to an unusual landscape feature, another variation on the theme of tree mountaineers: a mountain oak wood, a towering presence.

"Unusual" does not do it justice. It is a relic, a scrap of Lakeland's long lost mountain woodland. What you see when you stare up at those trees from Keskadale Farm is nothing less than living history. And to be clear, it is not the trees themselves that tower, but rather the whole wood. It is a wood of small trees as English oaks go, but the hillside to which it clings, a flank of Ard Crags, is perilously close to vertical. Silviculturists who specialise in the Atlantic oak woods of western Europe are apt to use language like "woodlands at the edge", and few of them are much edgier than this. These oaks are "tree mountaineers" in the most literal sense imaginable. They climb. They push themselves to the very limit of what is possible for oak trees in western Europe, and they do it for a living. Tiers of dark rock crags frowned down from within the trees, for what is not rooted oak tree there is bare rock. Even as the rain clouds began to relent and roll back uphill, they still didn't clear the top of the oak wood. Just how high did this wood climb? It reached for the sky, and for a considerable number of days in any one year the wood must be on first-name terms with it. The miracle of these trees – one of the miracles of these trees – is that they ever found sustenance on such a hillside, and they go on finding it. As tree mountaineers go, they are true professionals.

I stayed at the farm's self-catering apartment for a few days and asked about the wood and if I might walk up through it. I was advised against it simply on the grounds of the difficulty of the terrain and that my best bet was to climb the ridge of Ard Crags and look down on the wood from above.

The morning after that day of Moss Force in its "Shadow of God and the World" guise was plucked from another world of sunlit uplands, and the Shadow of God was mercifully elsewhere. At the top of the pass on the road between Keskadale and Buttermere, Moss Force was simply bright and beautiful. The rowans clustered around their high pool, their leaves gone, as you might expect in such an airy stance and November in full cry, but you might be surprised by the way they still clung to a blazing crop of berries, the reddest red in Lakeland's autumn. There is no hiding place for such a shade and the Scandinavian thrushes had found them: six fieldfares had paused there on their way south to richer pickings. Fuel for their journey, though.

Ard Crags derives its considerable charm from its situation. From the west, above Buttermere, it is a slender wedge
of a hill, a single curve that tapers as it climbs to a flattened double summit, hemmed in by mountains all round.
From the east, it opens magically into an apparently isolated
mountain, like something transplanted from Sutherland.
The illusion shatters as soon as you climb, however, for it
is hemmed in by mountains on every flank. But its modest
1,800 feet does not compromise its mountain-ness.

Two things happened on the summit. One was a flock
of more than fifty siskins. Siskins on a mountaintop: it's not
an everyday occurrence. The long grass and the heather on
the steep slope just below the summit ridge offered enough
seeds to detain them on their travels, but what were they
doing up there anyway? "…is less common on the ground
than most other finches…" intones the RSPB field guide,
so what does that say about this sizeable flock lingering on
ground that happens to be 1,800 feet up, and several miles in
any direction from the nearest spruce and larch plantations,
for a late autumn flock of siskins is much more likely to
descend on these, or the hanging bird feeders in your back
garden. Like the fieldfares on the rowans of Moss Force,
they can only have been birds on the move, snatching fuel
for the journey. Perhaps they were crossing from Newlands
to Buttermere via the valley of Rigg Beck, and a favourable
wind lifted them to the summit; perhaps the most experi-
enced birds had come this way before and knew about the
appetising grass and heather. Siskins often drift south in the
autumn, so these could have been Scottish birds making

way for their northern European kin, which often winter north of the border. When a siskin feeds on terrain like this, it flies in short and fluttery sprints and specialises in acrobatic landings. Multiply all of that by fifty-plus, paint it onto a mountaintop setting, and you have something to write home about.

Not the least of the glories of the spectacle is that when you lock your binoculars onto a small posse that has broken free of the flock and follow it across the sky, half the mountains of Lakeland blur out-of-focus through the background, and if you are slick enough with the focusing wheel to move from bird to mountains and back, you are witnessing a live documentary of nature that you will remember long after you have forgotten the details of every Lakeland set-piece mountain you ever climbed. You don't get this on Striding Edge. Even if you did, you would be so preoccupied with the mountaineering niceties of the next ten feet of ascent that you wouldn't notice. Right there is one of the reasons why this book won't be going to Striding Edge.

When I set out on what I thought would be a precarious journey – a Scot writing about Lakeland and daring to suggest that Lakeland could be wild, as well as Wordsworthian and Wainwrightian – this is exactly the kind of thing I had in mind: meeting the unexpected in the backwater landscapes of the range. It was never going to be yetis and snow leopards and grizzly bears, tigers or flamingos or the Serengeti (for these are the stock-in-trade of the world's nature documentary menus). It was never even going to be golden eagles, for 21st-century Lakeland is too overrun by

Homo sapiens for the comfort of *Aquila chrysaetos*. Rather, it would be a handful of fieldfares on a copse of rowans sheltering a waterfall pool from the fearful Shadow of God, or a flock of siskins breezing along a ridge in the middle of an airy whirlpool made from mountains.

Then, advancing a little down the dizzy tilt of land to the south revealed the top of the Keskadale oak wood, I thought of Coleridge again – *What a sight it is to look down on such a cataract...* – and a curious image slipped into mind, looking down on a cataract of trees. Yet so steep was the slope that there was no hint of what might lie beyond this upper frontier of England's Atlantic oak woods. The fact that the sight impressed me nevertheless was because of my sense of the wood from the farm, looking up – that and the fact that I know Atlantic oak woods in Scotland from Mull to Sutherland: the Keskadale oaks are among the more remarkable survivals. What proportion of people who walk to the summit of Ard Crags even notice the trees below their feet, far less wonder about them – how they have survived, how they continue to survive on such otherwise bare hillsides. I suspect that very indifference, coupled with the awkwardness of the terrain, are the reasons. There is nothing more than a nameless green smudge on the map, yet it is infinitely more impressive than the Borrowdale Yews whose name *is* on the map, just possibly because Wordsworth was there, and not here. Wainwright thought the Keskadale oaks a plantation to protect the farm from erosion, but they are much, much older than that, a fragment of a phenomenon that is in retreat all down Europe's Atlantic coast, from Norway to Portugal. If you walk further east along the summit ridge of Ard Crags, you can see a second fragment at Birkrigg on the far side of Rigg Beck. Writing in the *Journal of Ecology* in 1922, one W. Leach wrote that "Keskadale and Birkrigg could probably lay claim to be as nearly virgin in nature as any others in Great Britain".

* * *

All of the above, then, explains why on a morning of deep grey midwinter gloom enlivened only by the snow-bloated whiteness of the beck above Mungrisdale and its companionably Satchmo-esque song, I walked west into the hills, pausing often to scan the flank of Bowscale Fell in search of a third mountain oak wood, which I now knew to be "the current upper altitudinal limit for semi-natural ancient woodland in England". The language may be a bit of a mangling of English ("highest" would have done), but I am grateful to the paper that contained it, the proceedings of a conference in 2012 titled "Trees Beyond the Wood", organised by the National School of Forestry at the University of Cumbria. It was the chance discovery of this archive that sent me out to find Young Wood. With reference to Mr Leach's observation about Keskadale and Birkrigg, it had observed that "Young Wood could challenge them for the title of the most untouched woodland in England". It seemed suddenly important to know why.

January had the day by the throat.

What wasn't the faded green of old cabbage or that peat-stained white water was a variation on the theme of grey.

The light was an infusion of all of these shades, a light

that was almost ugly.

It had the air of a day that had just stopped raining and was just about to start again, but neither was the case, which was a shame because a good downpour might have cheered the place up.

There was no wind, so nothing moved but the beck.

Nothing sounded but the beck and the rhythm of these boots.

High up, where I had half-expected to see the wood, there was a long, narrow grey rock band, a broken crag fissured with gullies.

Sit. Think about this. Flask of coffee by the beck, coffee as unappealing as the light. Why do flasks always do that to coffee? Stare at the mountainside. Something moves across the crag, a wisp of broken cloud shaped vaguely like a woman in a long skirt. She dances slowly along the face of the crag, then her skirt snags on a rock and she stops.

Binoculars.

This is ridiculous. Binoculars to try and find an oak wood that should be, *has to be*, in plain sight. Start with the woman-cloud.

Disbelief.

That's it!

Not a crag fissured with gullies, a woodland; but a woodland unlike any other, trees as wispy and airily insubstantial as the woman-cloud's skirt.

What emerged in the binoculars were grey trees, spindly as skeletons, but wiry, whippy, loosely animated by the same breeze as the now shredded woman-cloud had been. In truth, they looked like nothing at all. From that distance and looking up 500 feet to the wood's nearest edge, it was as if every tree conformed to a kind of prototype, as if nature had predetermined what it would take for an oak tree to thrive 1,600 feet up a Lakeland mountain, which, as near as makes no difference, is where the "current upper altitudinal limit for semi-natural ancient woodland in England" has laid down its 21st-century marker. That combination of the airy nature of every individual tree, and the fact that they cram together as if there was nowhere else to go (yet how many miles must there be in all Lakeland of the 1,600-foot contour?) explains why, on such a grimly midwinter day, Young Wood is so difficult to pin down. It is almost invisible.

But suppose you had wandered this way on a bright midwinter day of sunlit snow and you chanced to look in the right place from below and, at a distance (the only way almost everyone sees it), you might see a mysterious intrusion into the free, smooth flow of the snow across the fell, something shrugged and crumpled, something that garlanded its portion of the fell with a hint of menace. If you were stop and give it a second glance (hardly anyone does, even when it is clearly visible), you might wonder what it could possibly be. And this is where Young Wood begins to get really interesting.

If your curiosity was sufficiently aroused, then, logic would suggest that you get out a decent Ordnance Survey map – say, Landranger 90, Penrith and Keswick – to see what it is and what it's called. Alas, the only thing it reveals is the existence of an enigma, not what it is or what it is called. It's not there. Maybe you are a fan of old maps and you like to carry one around with you when you criss-cross Lakeland to study the evolution of cartography as you go. This time, the old map wouldn't help you either. It's not on anyone's map and it never has been. "The most untouched woodland in England" and "the upper altitudinal limit of semi-natural ancient woodland" is simply not on the map.

I now know, thanks to a forced immersion into all things Lakeland, that many a Lakeland fell-walker would be unfazed by such a lapse, mutter a dark oath that contained the words "O.S. maps" somewhere in its midst, then they would simply produce a well-worn copy of the indispensable authority that has the answer to all problems pertaining to all things Lakeland, the Ghostbuster of the Fells, A. Wainwright. In this particular case, out would come his *Pictorial Guide to the Lakeland Fells, Book Five, The Northern Fells*. Straight away, No Name Beck suddenly has a proper name because Wainwright knew what the Ordnance Survey apparently didn't: it's called Bullfell Beck.

Now then, let's turn to his drawing of the flank of Bowscale Fell (the one where Young Wood is supposed to be), with its meticulous identification of the landscape features. There is the waterworks building and recorder apparatus (check: oh, that's what it is, is it?), there is the sheepfold (check), there is the East Ridge (check), and there is the hillside on which he notes "dead heather", "heather" and "grass". He describes four routes to the summit of Bowscale Fell, all of which should, in theory, provide clear views to the very spot of which the Trees Beyond the Wood conference offered what is surely a truly significant perspective in the history of the landscape of all Lakeland, all

The Tree Mountaineers (2)

England:

Looking down from the top of Young Wood, it is possible to say that everything below this point was once the wildwood of England.

But Young Wood is not on Wainwright's hillside either. You would have thought (okay, I would have thought, as an outsider and more of a Wainwright agnostic than a disciple) that if anyone's curiosity would be aroused, it would be his. The fact that it aroused mine instead can doubtless be explained away because I came with a nature writer's instinct, not a fell-bagger's or a guide-writer's. And it is easy to have a certain sympathy for Wainwright. Looking at the actual mountainside rather than a drawing in his book, scanning it in some detail with good eyesight and a sense of what I was looking for because I had already seen Keskadale and Birkrigg, and having scanned and seen nothing that looked like any oak wood I had ever seen anywhere, my first thought was this:

"So where the hell is Young Wood?"

Only the patient scrutiny of the hillside, then the woman-cloud and then the crucial assistance of good binoculars helped me to prise it free from its lair. That and the fact that my mission was not to climb to the summit of the fell by a recommended route, but rather to find Young Wood.

Having found it, it was time to get close. Easier said than done. Firstly, it was a *very* steep hillside that steepened as it climbed. Secondly, the underfoot conditions were awful, much of it long heather covering loose rocks and scree, and nothing remotely like a path. Going back down would prove even less fun than going up. Whatever else Young Wood may have going for it, it is certainly well defended by its situation. As much as anything, that may well explain its survival.

The weather closed in as I climbed. The wind picked up, laced with squalls. These intensified and joined forces with each other until rain simply thudded down the valley from the west. As I closed in on the wood, wind and rain and trees crackled, a warning against intrusion, eerie and unchancy. "Tree mountaineers": not for the first time, I acknowledged John Muir's facility for *le mot juste*.

There are moments when the methods I use in pursuit of a deeper connection with nature inadvertently acquire something of the primitive hunter, or at least how I imagine the primitive hunter might have approached the habitat of any particular quarry. The sensation that this awareness arouses is always the same: surprise. I never see it coming, but it occurs to me now that when it does arise it is often in circumstances of adversity. I have never been the species of hunter who stalks a creature with a view to killing it in order to eat it or wear its pelt (or both), but occasionally I become aware that I am stalking *something*, that my step has slowed, my awareness of my surroundings has become more acute. That awareness crept up on me as I closed in on Young Wood. The quarry I sought was its essence. Wordsworth would have used the word "soul" but it's a word that lies uneasily in my mind.

Then, a twist in the process: the sensation became not that of the hunter but of the hunted, that I was not so much closing in on the wood as being reeled in by it. Of being

lured. The ground was difficult, even treacherous and, as the
weather deteriorated, the sky fell and the only view was
down. Uphill and into Young Wood, the cloud ceiling was
nudging down among the highest trees, layering a grey roof
across the wildwood of all England. I had set out specifically
to find Young Wood. Having found it, nature closed off the
rest of the world to me so that there was only Young Wood,
and a Young Wood corralled by torments of weather. I con-
templated the notion that the wood resented my arrival,
but that its response was: "Okay, you want to know what it's
like, come on up, let's see what you've got."

Then the surprise: elation.

Elation at where I was, at what I had found, at the willing acceptance of the negotiating terms that nature had
imposed on the situation. I climbed a gate in a fence that
surrounded the entire wood and stumbled up towards the
frontier of trees, the hidden scree often subsiding underfoot
under the heather and grass, so that upward progress was a
lottery. But this was my world; this the company I choose to
keep when I go alone. These are my destinations, as others
go to mountain summits and poles. Right then, right there,
was a place on my own map of the world that simply felt
right. It had no name, no country, and as the cloud seethed
down and the rain drenched and the wind unbalanced the
elemental act of putting one foot in front of another, I felt
that rarest of things in the landscape, any landscape: belonging. I sat in the company of the nearest three trees. They
offered not a scrap of shelter. Their trunks were skinny,
they divided within two or three feet of the ground, they
grew more sideways than upwards. They writhed, flaying

each other with whiplash strokes. The entire wood bustled, blustered, seethed with raucous energy, a sight and sound every bit as compelling and invigorating as a waterfall. To sit there was to be in the company of primitive forces, of primitive creatures, and, briefly, to inhabit something other. I was alone in a high fragment of mountainside, walled and roofed and floored by thick, grey, cold, sodden cloud, and with three natives of that place for company, three ridiculous, glorious oak trees. It was as if nature had responded to my ambition for the day by excluding everything else in the world from this extraordinary moment of being in that extraordinary scrap of Atlantic oak wood, the better to taste its full savour. Then something fell into place.

When I embarked on this book's journey, my only idea was to seek out those elements of what Lakeland has become where true wildness endures. I keep being asked at talks and book festivals what wildness is, what wilderness is; and politicians in particular seem to think it demands definition in order to legislate. Yet it is the least definable concept on Earth. It is utterly nature's doing and quite beyond our capacity to judge and define, or for that matter our right to define, for we deny it breathing space at every turn and have done for millennia. At best, our awareness of true wildness – okay, my awareness of true wildness – is fleeting, momentary. A touch. Then gone. What lingers are the consequences of that touch. "The touch of the moment, the touch of the daylight on the dream," as the writer Margiad Evans put it. Sitting just inside the edge of Young Wood in that particular circumstance, that moment, that time and place, I touched wildness. Anyone who tells you there is nothing wild in Lakeland any more is quite wrong. But you have to want to seek it out. Otherwise, it won't come and find you.

I have no idea how long I sat there. Eventually I was shivering. That ended the moment. The wildness retreated. I stood, took a few coldly stiff steps downhill, turned to look at the trees again. Only once in my life had I seen trees anything like these, at Craig Fiaclach at slightly over 2,000 feet up in the Cairngorms. It is all that remains of Scotland's natural treeline. It's a few hundred yards long and comprised solely of Scots pines, knee-high trees that grow sideways in response to the regime of winds that hurtle down from the plateau lands between 3,500 and 4,000 feet. The oaks of Young Wood are their kin, the last survivors in all Britain of the tribe of tree mountaineers.

* * *

I was surprised there had been a fence. I would discover that it was the work of English Nature in 2008. The hope was that by fencing off the growing trees and a surrounding area of hillside, they would keep out the sheep and the deer and that Young Wood might begin to prosper again, to expand for the first time in who knows how many hundreds or thousands of years.

I went back in late May. Now that I knew what to look for and where to look, it appeared as a rippling green wave, a vitally alive curiosity, a benevolent, vivid intrusion on that high flank of Bowscale Fell. From below and in sunlight its full extent was clear, as was its fragmented nature. Once

I was inside the fence again, I started looking for the next generation of Young Wood young oaks. It had, after all, been twelve years since the fence went up. There was a quite a bit of regeneration – of rowan trees, which is not so surprising – but of new oaks I could find not a trace. I was reunited with the three trees that had so rewarded my midwinter climb, sat in warm sunlight, and I drew them, remembering. Now that the wood was in full leaf and I had a clearer idea of its extent and its setting, I saw that they were within the most densely wooded part of the wood, relatively speaking. I added a fourth tree to the drawing that seemed to belong to the grouping, but which simply hadn't registered with me in January, for even in this company it was a runt. But it seemed to my inexpert eye every bit as old and going nowhere as the others. I began to notice, too, that there were scattered single trees far from the dense heart of the wood, some of them several hundred feet higher up, and these too suggest that the wood was once much more extensive than it is now. Lakeland's obsession with sheep has a lot to answer for. But, despite the fence, something is stopping oak wood regeneration and it may be that the existing trees are not capable of producing acorns. In which case, might it be said that Young Wood is dying on its feet?

The introduction to the report of the proceedings of that Trees Beyond the Wood conference of 2012 observed: "If Atlantic oakwoods are woodlands at the edge, then Young Wood, which is very small, fragmented and vulnerable, is beyond that edge."

I kept hearing and seeing three – and only three – species of birds: robin, buzzard and willow warbler. The warblers intrigued me. Imagine, the whole of Britain at their disposal after a flight from North Africa and they settled for Young Wood, 1,500 feet up a Lakeland mountain. You would think they might have picked a softer option. But have they come back to the place where they were born, in which case, just how long has their wistful downward scale of a song graced these blasted acres? There is absolutely no way of knowing, for wildness keeps that kind of knowledge to itself. The buzzards were obviously up from the big firs in the valley, but the fact that they lingered suggested that the understorey was populated with enough voles and mice to make the trip worthwhile.

There would be a third visit to Young Wood in the early autumn of the following year. I wanted to see it in its autumn clothes, to catch the sense of this phenomenon demonstrating the one matter-of-fact trait that embraces all oak trees everywhere: it must change colour in the autumn and, as it did so, would its very presence be any more obvious as it dressed for autumn? Now that I knew what I was looking for, I saw it from two miles away, from the mountain village of Mungrisdale, and from the moment I stepped out of my car. It was caught between two diagonals, a wedge of hillside on the left and the edge of the dense canopy of a tree in the village on the right. The space between the two was filled with a piece of a flank of Bowscale, and its basic smoky brown shade of gone-over heather was broken by a broad and shapeless streak of something tinged green and yellow and orange. It took a moment for the significance of what I was seeing to fall into place. It was a slice of Young Wood. It took the vigour of that autumn shade to realise that it was visible from the village, not that any of Mungrisdale's visitors was giving it a second glance. It was the first time I had given serious thought to the village's situation.

Mungrisdale is out-on-a-limb Lakeland, with an agreeable frontier-town feel. I have always been drawn to edges in the landscape. The village clings on to the outside edge of Bowscale Fell, a north-east corner of Lakeland's northeast corner. To the east, the world is changed utterly. The land lowers then flattens. To the west, the world is all mountains; the land closes in, bears down, steepens mightily, soars. Hidden in the fells, but umbilically connected to Mungrisdale by the River Glenderamackin (and doesn't that sound Irish, like something you could step-dance to?), is one of those defining moments of local geography and geology that I love to stumble upon. It occurs high on Mungrisdale Common, between Bowscale Fell and Blencathra's almighty sprawl. There, two waters rise. One, Blackhazel Beck, flows north-west and straight into the River Caldew, which curves east, forsaking the hills, then curves north and heads for Carlisle. Yards away from the source of Blackhazel Beck, but on the far side of a watershed, a second water emerges, flows south-east, loops around the southmost thrust of Bannerdale Crags, heads north-east through the last of the fells until it suddenly swerves east to burst into Mungrisdale by the back door: the River Glenderamackin. Even now, after such diverging starts to life, the two waters are only a mile apart, but as the Caldew turns north, becomes lowland, the Glenderamackin declines to forsake the fells, heads south then west clinging to Blencathra's skirts, becomes the Greta at Threkeld and flows into the Derwent at Keswick.

In Mungrisdale, then, walking by the Glenderamackin, pausing at once to accommodate the realisation that I could see Young Wood from its single street, I fashioned a new connection with this land, a connection whose name was Mungrisdale, and the day gathered gravitas and a sense of mission about its shoulders. I like it when that happens. It has to do with tuning in to the landscape, of giving it time, of coming closer to the land itself. I looked up at Young Wood again and thought that if I had not already immersed myself in those lonely acres and someone asked me what I thought I was looking at, the last thing on my mind would have been oak trees.

The river dived down under Mungrisdale's stone bridge and between tall-treed rock walls, down through a gorge redolent with plump moss and white water and lusty riversong. The only creature that can compete with such a song is a dipper, one of the most endearing of hill-fellows-well-met wherever I find it, for it harks me back to the very earliest of all my explorations of the hills of home. Dippers sing in every weather and in every season of the year. Not only that, they appear to have evolved a technique of delivering song that cuts through the throat-iest, throbbiest outpouring of river and rock and makes itself heard. Perfectly on cue, such a song emerged from a moss-cushioned rock fifty yards upstream from the bridge. It carried as clearly as a skylark on a still spring morning. It posed on that dense green backdrop for just enough seconds to permit two photographs, the second not quite quick enough, a back view of a disappearing upstream blur. A finger hovered, pressed "delete". The blur vanished. But nature had already graced the day with its good omen.

The valley opened up west of Mungrisdale. The extrovert outcrop of Bowscale Fell called The Tongue heaved towards the village in huge curves, constricting the upper valley to half the width of the lower one. The first time I saw it, that frozen day up at Bowscale Tarn, it was elegant in new snow and sunlit. Among the photographs I took that day was one that placed the sweep of its lower slopes in a diagonal that bisected the frame, from high on the left to low on the right. Beyond it, The Tongue's shadow was cast on to the far wall of the valley, which, being south-facing, still accommodated a sunlit snow band along and just below Bowscale Fell's east ridge. But below that snow band and above the shadow of The Tongue was what looked like a rock band. Inadvertently, and in complete ignorance, I had taken my first photograph of Young Wood, without realising it was there, without knowing it existed, a state of affairs that put me on a par with – my best guess – ninety-nine per cent of fell-walkers who pass this way.

Fast forward to the following early October, then, the sun warm on the road by the river in Mungrisdale, and (such is the impression it has made on this wandering nature writer's mind) the first thing I had looked for was Young Wood, and there was a thrill of anticipation at the glimpse of it high on that wedge of hillside. And once the dipper had performed its greeting and once the village fell behind and the valley opened, there was the wood, lit from stem to stern and more yellow and orange than green. And yet it would be dishonest if I did not acknowledge that even in its early autumn prime it came as a hefty disappointment that it still clung to its mountainside with so little spectacle: no, with no spectacle of any kind. It still looked like nothing at all.

Turning away from the river, the climb began, easy enough at first with glimpses and earfuls of the beck that tumbles almost from Bowscale Fell's summit and more or less forever in the shadow of The Tongue, that beck the Ordnance Survey has not got round to naming yet. There's plenty of time, it's only been 10,000 years. The third climb up to Young Wood would prove to be the worst yet, having gathered every last resource of summer's growth to fuel its resistance. The heather was thicker and taller, between knee-high and waist-high. The gorse had prospered, bulked up, grabbed more land, blocked more gaps, sharpened every spike and aimed it carefully at me, every bush as tight-packed as spears in a schiltrom. You look for ways round them. There aren't any. Eventually you wade forward and upward as the mountainside steepens and steepens and you swear a lot. And somewhere down there, where your often unseen boots make contact with the raw stuff of the mountainside, you feel the buried surface of the scree slip beneath you, messing with your balance, which is already precarious enough on such a gradient. You lurch a step, grab at heather in the hope that it will hold you and save you from an awkward fall, but your hand closes instead on gorse. This (I am forced to remind myself every few minutes) is not a mountaineer's or a fell-walker's expedition, it is strictly a nature writer's, and we see the mountain differently and relate to it differently. Nothing else could account for it, nothing else could justify being right here, right now, intent on a wood that does not look like a wood, but nevertheless has a remarkable claim to fame. Not that it's famous. Relative relief on such a climb comes in the form of an outcrop of bare rock, because it is substantial, reliable, solid and utterly free of whins. But after the joy of a fifteen-foot scramble… more heather, more whins, more scree.

The passing glance won't accommodate it, and most fell-walkers don't even venture a passing glance, but there is a heart to Young Wood, where a small gathering of taller oaks rise above the dense growth of frontier shrubs. If you come on the wood from directly below, the tall trees are at the back, at the top; they beckon, still chanting their perpetual challenge: "Come on up, let's see what you've got." I aimed for that group of venerable ancients (I am guessing here, I have never seen oak trees like these anywhere else, their dimensions alone would suggest something around a decade old, but in this climate, these circumstances, they could be ten times that, or twenty times, or fifty…woodland as enigma). I reasoned that once I was in among the trees the going would be easier as I clambered up through the wood. I never got halfway. The word is "impenetrable". In this case, it is at its most literal. There is no way through here. I climbed as far up into the wood as I could, which was not far at all. The gradient reached as near vertical as makes very little difference at all, the same wretched blend of heather and hidden scree and bare rock prevailed, infiltrated the frontier trees, and these were so densely packed that their trunks overlapped and branches interlocked. You think, oak is solid stuff, the stuff of battleships and tables. I work on an oak table at home. It's a serious piece of wood. When a £20 million restoration of the Great Hall at Stirling Castle needed replacement oak roof timbers, they were sourced at Strathyre Forest just a few miles inside the Highland Edge; the trees were meticulously felled and hauled out by a team of specialist Clydesdale horses, magnificent beasts to deal with magnificent trees. But here, the trees are skinny and wiry, mostly about nine or ten feet tall. They are designed to repel, a true frontier.

Frontier. They threw the word in my face, seared it into my mind, not so much a border between landscapes or countries but between worlds, a change of planetary ambience. With the writer's unslakeable thirst for word-knowledge, I consulted my decrepit dictionary for help and unearthed the perfect definition: "the boundary between the known and the unknown". The innermost sanctum of Young Wood, just 1,600 feet up a Lakeland mountainside, is as unknown and unknowable a place as I have ever seen. Eyeballing it again, and for the third time in less than two years, it oozed hostility. I would not have been surprised if it had hissed. At the interface between the known and the unknown, the unknown appears like a wall, a wall from which trunks and branches project outwards, a consequence of their leaning stance to counter the gradient. The only reliable means of upward progress was to grab a handful of heather and pull. I have no idea what the breaking strain of heather is but it hauled my thirteen-and-a-half stones uphill without protest. Tree trunks are only more reliable if you can find one, and having found it, you can also reach through the cloying, whiplash branches. The whole frontier is an animated dance of warriors armed with many spears, warriors for nature. The trunks also divide chaotically from fat moss-drenched roots. The results are sprawling trees that interweave with other sprawling trees in every direction. I reached the second tier of trees only because the frontier yielded at one point to a bare rock. I scrambled up almost gleefully, but once I was on top of it there was nowhere to go in any direction other than back down the rock.

Young Wood is not a place to linger in any comfort. A narrow, heathery, rocky, scree-bottomed depression offered a compromise of a kind, both feet braced against the slope. It was hemmed in by trees, behind and on both sides, so the only view was down. The Bullfell Beck clings to the north flank of The Tongue for much of its short journey across the map of Lakeland, before curving round the foot of the slope to disappear forever into the River Glenderamackin, but its voice had underscored the entire climb, and it was still the dominant voice when I reached the first of the trees. The wind picked up suddenly to a stiff breeze, and that set the leaves of Young Wood sighing, their myriad twigs and branches and trunks rattling and creaking. There came a moment of transition in the day then, a moment when I heard the gentle crescendo of its speech achieve the precise volume of the now distant beck, an acoustic equipoise that made a single voice of wood and beck and neither stood out above the other; the two voices had become one, and together they spoke the language of the land itself. And there was another symptom of a nature writer's mountain expedition rather than a mountaineer's: I would leave Young Wood with the top 1,000 feet of the mountain unclimbed, but content that a summit had been reached. Not a summit of far-flung views, but rather one of insight, an enhanced understanding of the mountain's inscape that the Wainwright-ticking fell-walker hell-bent on the summit will never know.

Peering through the chaotic frieze of these oaks of unguessable pedigree, there was a glimpse of Young Wood's westwards sprawl across the flank of Bowscale Fell. It presents an extraordinary aspect. If you love trees and forests and lesser woods, and you love to see them interact with mountains (the south end of Ullswater, for example), then the westward view of Young Wood from within both astounds and dispirits at the same time. Something holds it in check above and below, its growth seems physically limited between a maximum altitude and – inexplicably – a lower one. What stops it from growing *down* the hill, especially now that a sheep fence protects it from grazing in every direction, offering it scope to triple its size at least? There again, the land is so steep and inhospitable to every plant other than heather and gorse that I wonder whether grazing was ever a serious factor in curbing its growth. For the bottom line is that it's an awful place to grow trees. Young Wood grows the way it does and looks the way it does because of where it is, and maybe it is as simple as that and maybe it always was. The two things I can't help wondering are:

Just how old is it, and, without help, just how long has it got left?

I reached out a hand to the nearest tree, as spindly and shapeless as all the others, and virtually trunkless, for it emerged from a moss-encased ground-level hub and instantly shot off in every direction. If it had been flowers, you would have called it a bunch. But the nearest offshoot of that hub was the thickest of the bunch, and when I closed my hand round it, it rocked with the impact. Oak trunks don't normally rock when you reach out a hand to them. Yet there was something in that untypical movement that was responsive, as if the oak in turn was reaching out to me as I had reached out to it. In its web of sunlight and shadow (so many skinny shadows from so many skinny limbs) and garbed in the turning overtures of autumn, the nature of that response lodged in my mind as a gentle rebuke. Why would that view westward, glimpsed between its many limbs that shimmied in the freshened wind, "astound and dispirit" at the same time? What was this tremulous movement that coursed through the tree but vital living evidence of its own wellbeing, its own spirit? Then just as suddenly, the rebuke had a voice I understood, a familiar form of words:

> *Move along these shades*
> *In gentleness of heart, with gentle hand*
> *Touch – for there is a spirit in the woods.*

I was learning that you are never too far from Wordsworth when you linger thoughtfully in these Lakeland fells.

Yet as things stand, Young Wood appears to be valued as more of a curiosity than anything else, or perhaps as a historical monument, but a monument to natural history. "The most untouched wood in England" is an accolade of a kind, but if it continues to be untouched and if the limit of the national park authority's ambitions for it is a sheep fence and then do nothing, then I am not at all sure that is an appropriate response. The very existence of this high-altitude oak wood, and the woods at Keskadale and Birkrigg, suggests that a much more widespread mountain oak wood once cloaked these fells. It is well worth exploring the possibility of restoring it, at least in part, of feeding the spirit in the woods. The valley above Mungrisdale is an oak wood waiting to be reborn, from the valley floor to the treeline, as defined by Young Wood.

★ ★ ★

Slithering back down towards the beck (the voices of the trees receding, the voice of the beck advancing, the old imbalance restored), I remembered something that happened when I had been there in May. I had stopped by the confluence of the beck and the river at the end of the day. I poured coffee and nibbled chocolate while I stared back up at Young Wood. Then I tried to imagine every slope of that box-canyon-like valley shrouded in low-to-the-ground oaks, the trees thickening about the beck and the lower slopes, burgeoning copses of rowans and birches, the whole awash with birdsong and May sunlight, cuckoos and ring ousels, red squirrels, pine martens, badgers, foxes, peregrines, goshawks maybe. In such a landscape, you might wander this way *en route* to one of the four options Wainwright lists for ascending Bowscale Fell, and you might pause and pronounce the place wild. I passed the time of day with a fell-walker with a Cumbrian voice, who had just descended by the far side of The Tongue. He caught my accent and asked what I was doing so far from home and with so many mountains in Scotland at my disposal. So I told him. Then, on a whim, I asked him if he knew about Young Wood. He shrugged. I pointed.

"What, *that*?"

"That. Survivor of the original wildwood, the summit of the Atlantic oak woodlands in all England."

"I had no idea. I've been here dozens of times."

He stared at its singularly unprepossessing presence, then he said again: "I had no idea."

Therein lies the reality for the tree mountaineers of our land. When it comes to looking after them and permitting them a future (a future they would have no trouble sustaining if it wasn't for our constraining presence on the face of the land), we have no idea.

Yes, these Lakeland hills have merit, and every now and then you come across the rarest, most precious of all their merits, which is that some of them are still surprisingly wild.

Five

The Juniper Belt

OTTER SIGNS BY THE RIVER, a perfect set of five-toed prints in a yard of bankside mud, a fish-bone-tattooed spraint from the night or the early morning on a prominent tuft of grass. Having seen the footprints, the prominent tuft was the obvious place to look for confirmation. Otters have habits. They leave messages where other otters can read them. I am not sure how he might feel about the allusion but there was something Picasso-esque about the arrangement of fish bones. Think of the hands of his blue period painting of the old blind guitar player. Look again at the fish bones in the otter spraint: two groups of bones oddly parallel, equally oddly shaped, like fingers. Ah, maybe you had to be there.

Goldrill Beck. There is poetry in this water too. Two soft syllables that fit well together then the decisive snap of "beck". Follow it with the word "otter" and you have the makings of haiku: the first line, the prerequisite five syllables. To a purist, the next line must have seven syllables, then five again to complete the verse, three ideas that together amount to a fourth, a portrait of a river. Something like this:

Goldrill Beck, otter,
Kingfisher flare, heron grey,
All bad news for fish.

Not the best haiku you ever read, but it's an entertaining game for one, walking beside quiet waters on a still and sunlit morning with no destination. It would be a particularly dull species of nature writer who failed to respond to a landscape graced by art and named by poetry, even if the name does actually mean "gold river river". From the front door of a favourite place to stay in this part of the world, called Old Water View (the beck flows past the door), to the east shore of Ullswater, water of one kind or another keeps you company for much of the way. This is as much a land of tarns and becks and waterfalls as it is of lakes and fells and oak woods. You fall in with one of these waters for a while and then you go your separate ways (the water tending downwards, the walker tending upwards, at least at this time of the day); long after you have parted company, its voice is still in your ears; its aura lingers, won't leave you.

The root of a young willow pushed out from the top few inches of the bank, a willow so young it had yet to decide whether to opt for girth or height. The root emerged in two short horizontals that quickly fused into one, so that it formed a triangle with the bank. These, and lesser, flimsier, rooty thrusts beneath had attracted the attention of a pair of common sandpipers with nesting notions. He was on a stone at the water's edge, agitated, fidgety, bouncy, calling, advertising himself and announcing the walker's intrusive gait for the benefit of his mate. She was not hard to find, silent and still in the nest. The pair had slung it snugly into the willow root, and against the soft earth shelf on which the base rested. It was untypical nesting terrain for sandpipers, which mostly incline towards a scrape in the ground lined with vegetation. But that inches-wide shelf in the bank and the ready-made walls of the root apparently offered a more appealing alternative. The nest fitted well for the moment, but next year or the next, that emergent root with its grey-green tassles of foliage will have consolidated into a trunk with designs on treehood. For the moment though, all was well in their world, apart from the walker who played games in his head with haiku and Picasso and a beck (which, in his head at least, he still calls a burn: he's still learning the language of this land) that lives up to its name on such a morning. Pure gold. Clear as the morning. The walker was charmed by it all, the male sandpiper on his stone more alarmed than charmed, unfurling his ritual disapproval. His anxiety took the form of a low circuit inches above the beck; wings stiff and fast, the shallowest of wingbeats, a constant quiver from quarter-past-nine-to-twenty-past-eight and back; the upper wings (long for the size of the bird and gently angled) a dark grey-brown meticulously decorated with thin, bright white flashes that match the angle of the forewings, solid white from body to mid-wing, then it frays to a series of perfectly aligned fragments that look like…well, fish bones. Then a glide, a tightening of the circle that ended back on the same rock where it had begun.

The call cut through the morning. Nature's voice proclaiming nature's place. A salutary note for the walker: go softly. Be more nature yourself. Be wilder.

★ ★ ★

Walking north up the east shore of Ullswater from Side Farm, a watershed-between-landscapes kind of place: the right fork heads south up the valley of the beck to Hartsop through oak woods, and your eyes are forever raised to a swathe of mountains from Fairfield to High Street above Haweswater, the swathe bisected by the Kirkstone Pass. But go left and the track takes you north into a land in thrall to Ullswater. Wandering boots were lured upwards onto the lowest slopes of Place Fell, lured in this particular case by an oddly beautiful grouping of big larches, big oaks, and Chile pines. The larches, decked out in that intoxicating young green that I have long since considered to be the true shade of any new spring, were as substantial as the oaks, and every bit as much at home in a Lakeland landscape as the oaks. We have moved a long way since Wordsworth rounded on the 18th-century foresters who introduced them here. (Actually, the Dukes of Atholl must take the blame: the second duke planted larches in 1738 by Dunkeld Cathedral in Perthshire and one of them is still there, all 105 feet of it; but it was the fourth duke who established the larch plantation – he planted seventeen million, and his passion caught on among Sasunnach landowners.) In his 1810 guide to Lakeland, Wordsworth first laid into the architecture of new houses, arguing that it should "admit of it being gently incorporated within the works of Nature..." before seguing neatly into his insistence that the same principle "should also be applied to management of the grounds and plantations, and here is more urgently needed...Larch and fir plantations have been spread not merely with a view for profit, but in many cases for the sake of ornament. To those who plant for profit, and are thrusting every other tree out of the way, to make way for their favourite, the larch, I would utter first a regret that they should have selected these lovely vales for their vegetable manufactory…"

We have since learned to love the larch, not least, I suspect, because, uniquely among conifers, it honours the seasons by turning gold in the autumn and shedding its leaves, by tholing the winter darkly elemental and naked, before re-igniting in spring again. And larches that have space to grow can grow old gracefully and assume shapes both mighty and balletic. It was larches like these, with the first flush of spring hanging about them like a pale green mist, that beckoned; they were the reason for edging away uphill from Ullswater's shoreline path. Sometimes on a day like this one, with no destination, that kind of unplanned diversion is all that it takes, and inadvertently, the day begins to take shape. As often as not, this is how I go to work.

The trees were a gathering, a lofty parliament assembled to debate centuries-old wisdoms and to uphold the laws of nature. There was an air about their small wood, a dignity, great trees at peace. I wondered what might unfold if I were to keep their company all day, to linger in their midst and see what might rub off, what wisdoms they might share. But now my day was otherwise aligned. Whereas from below that assembly of great trees offered the one obvious focal point, the world looked completely different from their uphill edge. Beyond the larches, the hillside opened and widened and steepened, a patchwork of rock and hawthorns with bright green leaves. I watched a green woodpecker head out from the topmost branches of the highest tree and lope airily northwards. The colour match with the new spring green of the larches was so perfect that I contrived the bizarre idea of the tree working up a design from its own foliage and giving it a bird shape, setting it free, so that it laughed with the sheer exhilaration of flight. Nature was playing games with me that morning. Or I was playing games with nature. Either way, it all helped to mould purpose into my day, to edge me a little closer into the embrace of the hillside, to lean a little closer to a mountain I hardly knew at all.

Two hundred feet higher, the slope was contoured by a much older path than the wide lakeside track, barely wide enough to be a dual carriageway for sheep, a much more organic passage across the hillside. Wild flowers gathered along its course: wood sorrel, violets, primroses, but the pick of the bunch was a tiny copse of starry saxifrage. Even the Latin name has a certain panache – *Saxifraga stellaris* – but it is out-panached by Gaelic: *Clach-bhriseach reultach*, the starry stone-breaker. The idea of the saxifrage tribe as "stone-breakers" is a wonderfully imaginative flourish. If you have binoculars slung around your neck when you come across them, get down on your knees and invert the binoculars, lower them until they almost touch the flower, see the miracle that unfolds: the pink sepals, the five petals each with two brilliant yellow spots, the red or yellow anthers. No one ever felt foolish or short-changed by getting down on their knees to get close to a starry saxifrage.

There was a roofless cave in the mountainside, guarded by a sentry-stone, a standing stone that simply stands of its own accord rather than one that our ancient ancestors stuck in the ground, and with a split in the top. It looked as if it had been cleaved by a battle-axe. Doubtless there is a legend thousands of years old to account for its solitary stance at the mouth of the cave, a legend that may also account for the ash tree that now commands the space within the three cave walls that remain. Because its natural growth was constrained by the rock walls, it sent five tight-packed trunks vertically upwards seeking sunlight, and one horizontal limb much more massive than the trunks out through the cave mouth into the daylight where it forked and prospered and spawned new branches in a series of upward curves. But would the legend then explain the holly tree that found the arrangement to its liking, rooted in the darkest recess at the back of the cave so that it crept up the wall there, and as it grew it began to thatch the five trunks in such a way that it created a kind of dented dome, which is how the cave gained a new roof?

The morning warmed. I sat on in the shade of that extraordinary chamber, sketching, making notes, marvelling at nature's capacity to adapt constantly and reinvent itself. A persistent voice scored almost that entire and delectable hour. It was another Lakeland wren. The mountainside patchwork of piled rock and screes and hawthorn tree seemed to work well for wrens wherever I walked (I lingered over a theory about the merits of living in a thorn-guarded nest) and now there was one that was clearly nesting in the gloomier depths of the holly (its prickly leaves a variation of the hawthorn's thorns). The wren's morning was a constant series of journeys from the holly to the screes and hawthorns, and to the standing stone, which was clearly a favourite song perch. It seemed to sing at the mountain, like Sparky, the American boy who used to sing to a mountain because the mountain would echo his song and send it back. *Sparky's Magic Echo* was a fixture of my childhood radio listening. One day the echo fails and a frantic search to find it begins. Finally the wise owl tells him the Old Man of the Mountain knows where it is and, sure enough, he knows that it was trapped in a cave, and he rolled away a stone from the mouth of the cave and Sparky and his echo were re-united. They don't write them like that anymore, but there it is to this day, immortalised with its own cartoon out there in cyberspace on YouTube.

Back in the 21st century, other bird voices drifted dreamily across Place Fell as the heat built. The clamour of Canada geese, softened by distance, thermalled cheerfully up from the lake. I seem to be in a peculiarly small minority because I like Canada geese. They are big and bold and handsome and their voices and their skeins keep me going between early spring and early autumn when the Greenlanders, the Icelanders and the Scandinavians among the wild goose tribes have gone home from these islands to breed and touch base with the sense and the scent and the belonging of their homelands around the Arctic rim. I envy them their far north springs and summers. I welcome them back when September's vanguard and October's hordes write their stories all across my northern skies, northern but sometimes not northern enough to feed my instincts. Until September, then, I have the Canadas.

They were originally incomers, of course – but then, weren't we all? Now, the Canadas are no more aliens than larch trees. For no good reason, they were freighted from the New World in the 18th century in the holds of transatlantic clippers, which is a strange way to cross an ocean for a bird that is perfectly capable of crossing it under its own power. They became desirable ornaments for the gardens and domestic-sized lakes of big houses across England, and the Victorians with their gruesome take on the Scottish Highlands took them north to add to their peacocks and black swans and other showy creatures that never belonged there and never wanted to. But being geese and both resourceful and adaptable, the Canadas thrived, and of course they escaped from lives of wing-clipped, show-off-accessory servitude to reclaim a new kind of wildness in the country that was foisted upon them, and now they are home birds and here to stay whether the human descendants of their captors like it or not.

And now that I was done with Sparky, it was Thoreau's ghost that came to me with the Canadas:

In the morning I watched the geese from the door through the mist, sailing in the middle of the pond, fifty rods off, so large and tumultuous that Walden appeared like an artificial pond for their amusement. But when I stood on the shore they at once rose up with a great flapping of wings at the signal of their commander, and when they had got into rank and circled about over my head, twenty-nine of them, and then steered straight to Canada...

Our Canadas have had the migratory urge more or less knocked out of them. There is some local movement to low-lying ground in winter, and large moulting flocks form in the east-coast firths of northern Scotland, which include many birds from the north of England. But it's not like going back to Canada from Concord, Massachusetts, which is what Thoreau was witnessing. And on the west coast of America, migration from Alaska and southern Canada to Mexico is routine.

Something fundamental is lost whenever and wherever human behaviour deprives a wild creature of its natural instincts; something cruel creeps into our tendency to brand the results as "pests", which is the fate of Canada geese in parts of Britain where they thrive, where the people's disapproval is articulated by men with guns. In that undignified process, our species denies the unpalatable truth that it's the people who are the pests.

For the moment, and like the groves of larch trees on the slopes of Place Fell, the Canada geese make an agreeable contribution to the 21st-century biodiversity of a Lakeland morning. I was glad of them. I caught in the binoculars a skein of around a dozen as it fashioned a wide, sunwise circle in the airspace above the southern end of Ullswater, then pitched towards the surface and a raucous welcome from more of their kind by the reedy shore, the reunion itself screened by trees. The spectacle and the soundtrack fitted the landscape well enough.

Other voices drifted up and across the hillside. Stillness increases your capacity to listen as well as see. A single curlew, northing, the sun on its back as it flew fifty feet below the path lit vivid lights in the spearhead-shaped slash of white that extended part way along its back from the white rump, the spearpoint as fixed on north as a compass; and all the while it called out its own name with its oboe voice. There is nothing about a curlew that isn't wild, isn't beautiful, isn't somehow affecting, harking you back to long-lost times and places, urging you forward to new times and places just beyond the horizon. And there is always in my mind an old association between curlews and bog myrtle, not an obvious one perhaps, but one that that settled agreeably there through a poem:

Bog myrtle smells
like curlews sound,
curved pibroch of scent
low on the moor, clinging
to legs and trailed fingers,
tangible as summer rain
but sweeter, sharper, wilder,
headier a brew,
beloved of argus wings
drinking only in sunlight
and thirsting
in scented shadow.
Brushing by,
we also drink in –
scent, sound, sunflier –
bending low,
curved as curlews

Coal tits and great tits bustled in and out of the cave mouth, singly and in courting pairs, diving down into the holly, confiding to each other in whispers and insistent chatter. The nearest brushed by a couple of feet away. Stillness also admits you in on such tiny theatres of nature. And whenever I raised my head and looked beyond the enclosing confines of the cave and its trees, Fairfield and Hart Crag clasped their skylines together in the south and south-west. There are many theatres of nature in such a landscape.

Without getting up, I found a piece of scree that looked like the outline of the Old Man of Hoy, a giant sea stack in Orkney if you don't know him. I thought I might take it with me as a souvenir, so that when a little time and distance had elapsed and I was back in the room where I write, I would find it among notes and sketches and photographs and maps and reference books, and its touch would help me to recall this here and now. But then I changed my mind, for it was where it belonged, a fragment of the fell, and I made a life-size drawing of it instead by laying it on the page of a sketchbook and drawing round it…drawing made easy. It may sound a pointless exercise, but it was a gesture, one more small connection with the landscape. In many ways my working life is a conglomeration of thousands of such gestures in dozens of landscapes, the sum of which strengthens the bonds and reduces the distance.

Eventually, I had to prise myself out of the cave, for I had become comfortable and at ease there, thinking my way into its landscape and writing it down. I climbed away from the path, among hawthorns that grew as often as not out of screes and gatherings of bigger rocks, so that the trees were thrown against the sky or sprawled awkwardly on the steeper slopes, just enough of them to insist that the climbing was a thing of constant diversion. You could hardly call hawthorns beautiful – they are too wiry and shapeless, and their skeletons show through. Even when they drown themselves in shaggy fleeces of late-spring flowers, they look more shaggy than shapely. But wild, absolutely wild, a gift for small nesting birds, and better equipped in the arts of tree mountaineering than anything else. *Almost* anything else.

The hawthorns thinned out with altitude, only to have their place taken by juniper. Place Fell's juniper belt does not announce itself with a hard frontier line across the mountainside, but rather with a few stunted outliers. It gives the appearance of being upside down. The higher you go, the more dense and impenetrable the gatherings, thicket, groves and swarms. You would think it should be the other way round. But it takes only a short uphill plod flummoxed by all-pervasive screes from those first outliers until you find yourself surrounded, and picking an upward route becomes maze-like, as well as steep and uneasy under-foot. Mountain screes are tricky enough without this. But the juniper's presence on that flank of Place Fell quickly becomes a head-high, interwoven forest where nothing else grows. *Almost* nothing else.

There is one extraordinary sycamore.

It is not tall as sycamores go, but this high on a Lakeland mountain you would not expect it to be tall. On the other hand its canopy is about sixty feet in diameter, its trunk ten feet in girth and quite massively rooted to compensate for being planted (by *what*? by *whom*?) in nothing more than a tumbledown morass of mountain rock more than 1,000 feet up. What is truly remarkable about it – apart from the sheer amazement you register that it is here at all – is the manner in which the juniper defers to it, forming up in a respectful guard-of-honour-like circle all round it and just beyond the reach of its canopy's shade when the tree is in full leaf. Not one twig of juniper dares to exploit that hallowed circle. Instead, the sycamore's shade confers a unique micro-climate on the portion of mountainside in its care, and smothers it in a shade of soft green you find nowhere else on that mountain at that altitude or anywhere near that altitude. Grass and moss, lush and rich and fertile and beautiful. Here I sat again to savour the atmosphere of another extraordinary tree mountaineer, and here I whiled away another hour or more, writing and looking round and grafting myself a little more securely into the realm of a singular Lakeland mountain. I had to stop halfway through because I like to use a fountain pen when I write (it's what works for me, it's as simple as that) and it had dried up, so I had to change the cartridge. My backpack is one of the few in the land that carries a packet of five cartridges, and if I were a betting man (I'm not) and if I could ever lay my hands on serious money (I'm a nature writer, that's never going to happen), I would bet serious money on this: that in the century or so that sycamore has stood on that mountainside, mine was the first ever fountain pen cartridge change ever to have been effected under the shade of its canopy.

A chaffinch and – almost inevitably – one more wren came and sang for me while I sat and wrote, and a male bullfinch that glowed a sumptuous deep pink perched on the topmost frond of the nearest juniper to the edge of the enchanted circle and delivered a soliloquy of soft, wood-wind notes that made me think of an old wooden flute. I nodded appreciatively and in turn to all three, and I alerted them to the skyline presence of a pair of peregrine falcons, not that I imagine they were unaware of them, but it seemed like the least I could do.

I was slowly getting to know this hillside, that lake shore, so I had been looking for the peregrines with a rough idea of where to look for them. There is something reassuring about the moment when a new landscape begins to repay early attempts to familiarise yourself with it, a moment when the process suddenly begins to work both ways, a moment when nature makes a positive movement in your direction. On an April day on Place Fell, that moment took the shape of a peregrine falcon, and apart from anything else it offered a reassuring echo of that rainbow-lit omen on High Rigg more than a year before. It was the smaller male that circled out from the skyline ridge while the female flew on, throwing a harsh scatter of syllables over her shoulder. The exquisite aesthetics of the peregrine do not extend to its voice.

The circling bird leaned into the rocks, folded its wings and poured itself 300 feet down the hillside, opened its wings wide and effected a U-turn that stalled into a perfect landing, perfectly lit. It was enough. The chaffinch, the wren, the bullfinch saw that all right, silenced themselves, vanished.

The first thing was the yellow. Three vivid sparks of it lodged in the blue-grey of rock and bird: the forehead immediately above the dark down-curve of the upper mandible, and the shins and ankles and splayed feet. If I had not seen the stoop and the air-braking turn and perch, if the bird were already there when I looked up, without the yellow, would my sweeping glance have brushed past it to search the skyline?

Settle. Steady the binoculars. Drink in the moment. Commit it to memory. Commit this:

Solid, muscly bird, unlike the slenderness of kestrel, merlin; the pose instantly restfully erect but with the illusion of a slight forward tilt, alert, ready, always ready; sunlight aslant on its stance, head in sunlight, slightly raised, the black-eyed falcon stare (the thinnest of yellow rims encircling it) was to the sky; the jet-black eye patch was a thickly inked-in Y-shape that extended down the white neck; breast and upper legs meticulously streaked black on white; head and one folded wing a lustrous dark blue; even folded the wings are primed, honed, sculpted instruments for a masterclass in the art of flat-out; the curve and taper of the nearer wing – oh, surely beauty and lethality were never more thoughtfully wedded than in nature's design of the peregrine wing; the further wing, the left one, defined by a midnight blue wedge of shadow against the breast; beyond the shadow a glimpse of more streaks, black on the whitishness of the coyly revealed underwing; the further wing held not against the body but slightly loosely; the right wing, you now realise, has masked that same looseness; tail short and blunt and the same mix of black streaks on white and dark blue, with a further echo of that midnight blue shadow.

Commit all that to memory to honour the moment

when nature leaned closer here.

Just before it flew, its mate gave voice again, its head swivelled, the stare now upwards and behind. Whatever its message, the raucous cry produced an instant response, for the male dived away downhill and so low to the slope that it was lost among junipers. High above, the voice of the female brayed harshly on and on.

★ ★ ★

It has been clear from early in this book's journey that trees would play a significant role. Tree mountaineers don't have it easy. They deal in survival against the odds. From the broken-open Borrowdale Yews to Young Wood's high-altitude, low-centre-of-gravity oaks to the rock-rooted hawthorns of Place Fell or Mardale Head, they push the boundaries of what is possible in the way of sinking roots and sowing seeds. Time and time again I have been brought to a standstill in humbled confrontation with a tree that appears to outwit the mountain (even the mountain's limitless repertoire of winds) so that time and time again I am helpless before the same two questions: "from where do you get the nerve?" and then "from where do you find the sustenance?" John Muir, who provided me with the concept of the tree mountaineer in the first place, said of the Sierra juniper that it was "seemingly content to live for more than a score of centuries on sunshine and snow...their stiff, crooked roots grip the storm-beaten ledges like eagle's claws". I am not sure about this, but I think that this solitary sycamore demanding its own inviolate circle of space, and holding the seemingly unstoppable swarm of the juniper belt at bay, might just be the noblest tree mountaineer in all of Lakeland.

Six

Time Stalls, You Grow Still, You Go Deeper In

A DAY OF LOW CLOUD that would spend the day getting lower: its effect was to push me down to the path along the shore of Ullswater. I'm a sucker for a good there-and-back walk because as the direction of travel changes, so does everything else, and as the day unfurls so does the light; so I set out from Patterdale to walk north as far as the day permitted then back again, to take my time and to feed into the journey scraps of old days and half days spent along the track, days spent loitering without intent, adding new layers of awareness to my slowly growing awareness of Ullswater – where it lies, how it lies, the lie of its land, who and what its natural neighbours are. By this time, I had won a degree of familiarity with Ullswater and its shores and surroundings, its lowland-into-highland embrace which I value so much from my work in Scotland. I liked the idea of a stretch of land and water that might emerge in my mind as something emblematic of the particular Lakeland I sought.

A barn with a crow-stepped roof interrupted the flow of the shoulder-high pathside wall, stone as grey as the greyest cloud and then some, but the roof eclipsed it with its daring duvet of thick moss, the only vivid shade in the landscape that sodden, hodden-grey morning. There were slates under there but the moss was wall-to-wall and skirt-to-ridge and it coated every crow-step on both gable ends. Wren and robin breakfasted there. The robin flew to the top crow-step and paused, to the ridge and paused, to the top crow-step on the other side and paused, and fed with every pause. Minutes later the wren arrived, used the crow-steps like a staircase, just as the barn's builder intended, albeit a staircase for generations of farm-workers to maintain the roof was what he had in mind; how long since that happened? Long enough for the moss to move in and settle and transform the entire roof from slate grey to moss green. The wren saw the crow-steps through different eyes from both builder and robin, and what it saw was a staircase of breakfast tables. The surface of every crow-step wore smooth moss like carefully tended turf, untrampled except by wren footprints, and these are gentle in their impact. The wren landed on the bottom step, having flown from the top of the nearby wall. A brief stillness, side-headed. Then a lunge…at what? What minutiae of a mountainside ecosystem live on the moss-cushioned crow-steps of an old stone barn? The next step was reached in a minute blur of minute wings, a vertical take-off followed almost instantly by a precision landing…precisely on the cliff-edge of the step. There were nine crow-steps. Every one was explored and plundered, a practised routine flawlessly executed. At the top, a snatch of song from an airy perch, suggesting a territory was still being defended, for all that the day lay on the cusp of autumn-into-winter. Theory: as the weather gets cold and insect life gets scarcer, the comparative warmth of the comparatively low-lying moss sustains more insects than most Lakeland mountain habitats. So, moss-on-stone, especially stone as level and easily worked as this, becomes central to small-bird survival. In my chosen portion of Lakeland, I have become more and more impressed by built stone that has become landscape itself, that has been given nature's blessing and folded into the lives of countless creatures, small mammals as well as small birds and insects. Field edge, lane, wood, beckside, lakeside, mountainside – the builders had a sure eye for their landscape as well as their raw materials, and what are their raw materials but the rock and the wood of their own place on the map?

Most barns hereabouts are on sloping ground. This one, with the crow-steps, was typical. The path is on a higher level than the field; the field slopes steeply down to the water's edge. The barn is built at the top of the field, and gable-end-on to the path. But the gable that rises from the edge of the path is about half the height of the gable end at the far end of the barn, where the wren hunted: nine chunky crow-steps at that end, ten much shallower crow-steps at the pathside end. But the ridge between the two gables has to be horizontal. And I am willing to bet there was no architect's plan, maybe a rough sketch, but mostly the eye and the sure hands of the builder, the floor worked into two or three different levels. It is a great compliment to nature that the builder built so well and so thoughtfully; it is a great compliment to the builder that nature embraced his work.

For a few moments, robin and wren occupied opposite ends of the ridge. I imagined they must know each other, that they must be part of each other's landscape. Seconds

later, the ridge was birdless. Each had dived into cover in
very different ways. The robin seemed to step off, fold his
wings and go into free-fall, cutting a peregrine-esque
diagonal across the path to vanish into a holly bush. Again,
the wren was a blur of wings, this time to execute a tight
loop back in towards the wall, where it squirted deep into
its gloomy, stony sanctuary. Seconds after that, a male sparrowhawk circled idly fifty feet above the barn, slate-blue
back, orangey barred front catching the light as it changed
course with half a dozen wingbeats and glided speculatively
out across the field, a pocket-sized predator whose yellow
eye glared into my binoculars. Its sudden presence in the
midst of what a moment ago had been empty air was an
exclamation mark on the unfinished page of my day. And
wren and robin would see that differently too, for the hawk
must also be part of their landscape, just as small birds diving
for cover in their various ways must be part of the hawk's
landscape a hundred times a day.

★ ★ ★

Across Ullswater, Catstye Cam scintillated: the forward-thrust,
eye-catching mountain-child of its vast and unlovely parent,
the massif of Helvellyn. Clouds heaved among the mountains that morning and glowered down on Ullswater, a
riot of colours, every one of which was a shade of grey.
Such a skyscape cast Catstye Cam in the role of disembod-
ied ghost mountain, blurred at the edges by sleety squalls,
weirdly afloat, hypnotically afloat. I first became aware of
Catstye Cam's allure one winter day when its handsome

pyramid, as viewed from more or less right there on the Ullswater path, was set off by snow corries on either side, the snow also hanging in drapes from the ridge of Helvellyn. Rainclouds drifted along the ridge so that yet again, the dark pyramid, not high enough for snow that day, stole the show. I photographed it with a telephoto lens from three miles away, isolating it with wooded foreground diagonals and the hung sheets of old snow, pictures that helped me to commit it to memory, because composing them helped me to *see* it better. With mountains – especially with mountains – size isn't everything.

For a moment, it put in mind the view of the Cairngorms massif from Gleann Einich, where a solitary walker's sensibilities can sometimes feel brutalised by the sheer bulk of Beinn MacDuibh and the corrie-sculpted walls of Braigh Riabhach, both of them over 4,000 feet; but how willingly your eye distracts to settle on the free-standing pedestal of Carn Elrig. And the summit of Carn Elrig is also the perfect viewpoint from which to consider the raw might of those huge plateau lands, yet it is not much more than half their height. Catstye Cam is a mountain in the Carn Elrig mould, which is the highest of compliments in my book. It may not be just as free-standing, given that Swirral Edge anchors it umbilically to its parent, but from various sightlines, and especially from the path along the east shore of Ullswater, it is unarguably a thing of beauty.

The lakeside path opened and closed sightlines as it rose and fell. Suddenly Catstye Cam was there again after a short absence, this time framed within the limbs and trunks of a cabal of Scots pines on a knoll above the lake, the darker because they appear against the sky. Anything that darkens Scots pines has the curious effect of making them more luminous, so that the greenery sings with a bluish edge, the bark reddens. There is no such thing as a dull day in the company of Scots pines. Here, the tallest of the group was also the slenderest. All its energies seemed to have gone into achieving height, for it had no canopy to speak of and it branched at six different levels, each clearly defined by space. In such distinguished mountain company, that singular tree held its own and with some panache. The grace and bearing of its stance were qualities to pause for and admire, not least because the path comes on it from below, then ascends the knoll it crowns; only the dullest of souls trudges on regardless. It is an ill-considered schedule or an ill-formed philosophy that fails to accommodate the leisure to linger before such a tree, for it is every bit as much Lakeland as lake or fell or beck or tarn or waterfall. For the seeker after wildness, it is as defining a landmark as the handsome mountain across the lake. It is a totem, a sacred gesture of nature; and even if you value nature only for what you can get out of it, then you could still argue that it was planted and raised in order that all who pass here might pause and take stock of the place where they stand and remember its capacity to soothe souls. In *The Native Pinewoods of Scotland* (Oliver and Boyd, 1959), the authors and foresters H.M. Steven and A. Carlisle offered three reasons for cherishing and safeguarding the future of the pinewoods, reasons that are just as relevant to Lakeland as to any of Scotland's mountain realms:

First, they are the authentic home of the distinctive strain of Scots pine at the western extremity of its natural distribution...Secondly, the native pinewoods are one of the most interesting survivals of our native vegetation...There is now general recognition in all civilised countries that such survival should be preserved on an adequate scale and it would be a national loss if those pinewoods were allowed to disappear... Finally, they can be considered to be not the least important of the historical monuments of Scotland.

The pinewoods that preoccupied them and inspired the book may have been on a different scale from that small herd of trees on their knoll above the Ullswater shore, but the essential principles are the same. There are groups of naturally occurring Scots pines all across Lakeland, they belong as indisputably to this landscape as to Rothiemurchus or Glen Affric or Torridon or other Scottish strongholds, and they too are at the western extremity of their natural distribution, likewise the Atlantic oak woods and their extraordinary Lakeland echo at Young Wood. And if you prefer your historical monuments tall and elegant and gilded with natural grace, rather than herded and stunted like the Young Wood oaks, then right there above the shore of Ullswater is a historical monument whose status is indisputable.

There was a juniper bush down by the shore, so close to the water's edge that it must surely wade from time to time. After days scrambling and contouring among the junipers high above the mountainside hawthorns, it was a surprise to see one in such a situation. There was a sudden brief blaze of sunlight on the water, and looking down at the bush in binoculars from the path a hundred feet above, it was set not against the mountainside but the brightening water. Its very stance recommended it. But so did its shape. From a central root its angled trunks opened and spread evenly to north, east, south and west so that it created the illusion of an organism in perfect balance. The odds of a juniper bush of all things growing like that are so long that it was worth a closer look. As I descended the scrubby hillside, I remembered something of English tree specialist Hugh Johnson's observations on the subject in his book *Trees* (Mitchell Beazley, 1973; Octopus, 2010).

Junipers, he said, do almost the exact opposite of most conifers: conifers grow fast, junipers are snail-slow; conifers like shelter, junipers like the south-facing slope (this one is on a south-west-facing slope) and "unmitigated light". Most conifers like leaf mould, junipers like mineral soil, or in this case, virtually no soil at all, a crack between stones, an unwelcoming tilth for more or less everything apart from juniper. It proved to be the most conspicuous bush in a small shoreline community of rock-rooted junipers, all of them similarly shaped apart from one extraordinary variant. It was a perfectly circular dish, about five feet in diameter and perfectly flat, as if it had opted for ground-cover rather than altitude. Yet nearby was another variant, a ten-foot-tall juniper tree so shapely and tapering in its tiers of growth that it could have doubled for a Christmas tree; so dense was the foliage from ground level to the topmost shoot, where you would hang the star, that there was no hint of anything that looked remotely like a trunk. The blue-grey waters of Ullswater shone through the spaces between the tiers of foliage. The effect was beautiful – a beautiful juniper tree, who would have thought it?

The rockfall that sustains this little shoreline community, long since consolidated into the shore of the lake, is a collection of huge boulders and slabs. It eludes me how the junipers contrive to mine the crevices and find the wherewithal to survive and, apparently, to thrive. It commands my admiration. We tend, as a species, to see nature as a bounteous provider without limits; not here, she isn't, not where Lakeland juniper is asked to burrow down into a landform you and I would consider unburrowable. So the evidence of my own eyes and the testimony of authorities including Hugh Johnson would seem to suggest that here lies the juniper's natural habitat, from Ullswater shoreline to high on Place Fell, and all of it as thrawn a sphere of cultivation as you or I might imagine. Yet consider this from Seton Gordon's *The Cairngorm Hills of Scotland* about what was revealed when an area of pinewood in Glen More was felled in the early 1920s:

The felling of the trees has brought into prominence the junipers of Glen More…the plants grow into small shapely trees, some of them 15 feet in height….In April 1925 on the south shore of Loch Morlich, I passed an unusually shapely juniper. It was tree-like in habit, resembling a thuja in its shape, and was approximately 24 feet high.

Thuja is a member of the cypress family, like juniper, and native to the Pacific Northwest, where John Muir christened the Sierra juniper a "tree mountaineer" and set in motion for me a train of thought, which, as you can see, has not yet run out of steam.

The following day, alternating between the lakeside track and the higher path that contours Place Fell's lower slopes, I found one more variant. True, it was a repeat of the disc configuration, but this time it was inverted so that it curved downwards. It had also been hoisted a dozen feet in the air because the cleft where it had rooted was on the top outside edge of a rocky outcrop.

A drab morning suddenly turned vile. A sodden gale charged down from the Kirkstone Pass, flayed the slopes of Place Fell and roughed up the surface of Ullswater into a ferment of whirlwinds and white horses. Suddenly it felt as if I was in the wrong place at the wrong time. Before the weather broke I had been sketching a birch tree whose infancy had clearly been so constricted by rocks just above its roots that the trunk bent to overlap one particularly triangle-shaped rock, which presented to the downhill view something that resembled the end piece of a bar of Toblerone. As the girth of the birch trunk had thickened over the years it had split to accommodate the ridge that (on a bar of Toblerone) leads to the gap before the next piece. By now I had begun to make something of a study of rock-rooted Lakeland trees, stopping to examine how they always adapted to the twist of fate that dropped the seed that spawned the root that became sapling in an awkward and gloomy tree nursery for one. But this was a new technique. It looked painful. But the birch's companion in that crazy paving of mountain rocks was the juniper with the downturned dish. As the weather worsened, I realised that the rock that accommodated the birch, and the neighbouring and much larger rock that accommodated the juniper, offered me comprehensive shelter – a backrest and windbreak in the rocks, and a canopy in the widespread, parasol-like dish of the juniper. There, in much greater comfort than I had any right to expect, I ate lunch while I watched the storm cram the airspace above the lake with gusts and sleety salvoes of vicious weather. A kind of perverse contentment crept into the hour. Just like the trees, I had made an accommodation with the rocks, even if its duration was that of lunch break rather than life-times, as it is for the trees.

So often, the nature writer's only task worth the effort is to become nature. Watch and be, and write down what unfolds in that particular collision of time and place while you are there, while the very landscape is your host. Here, for example, I had just been presented with a glimpse of what it takes to dig into that mountainside. So my job became to root thoughtfully there, to tap into its every resource so that I might make the most of the moment, just as it is the job of the birch, the juniper, the Toblerone rock. Become nature. Become landscape. Take root for as long as nature requires it of you, for as long as nature permits it. Think of yourself as being that kind of native, however briefly; ingest its life-giving qualities so that understanding grows within you, the way the sap rises in that rock-hugging birch; so that some bright tomorrow when you come back to that particular Lakeland landscape, you can glance up from the lakeside path to where a birch and a juniper bask in sunlight and warmth and all is well with their world and you can feel kinship, because you were granted that glimpse of what it takes to hold your own on that hillside, to make accommodation with those rocks for the right to live with some dignity, and yes, with beauty.

Time stalls, you grow still, you go deeper in.

* * *

The mountains across the lake receded deeper into cloud, the wind eased down a notch, now layers of rain swept the west shore in veils hung from the heights, trailing their hems on the surface of the lake, the frailest of veils, the flimsiest of showers, but relentless. Distance diminished, grew insubstantial. Meanwhile the foreground advanced, clarified, pushed itself uphill towards me, demanding attention, because usually its voice is drowned out by the mountains. That foreground lay steeply downhill, took the form of more big larches, autumn shaded but fading from gold to antique amber, yet contriving in the day's pervasive and wan grey light to intensify their shades. They were corralled by a drystone wall about five feet tall, neatly curved around the outer flank of the group, dignifying and deferring to its landscape almost as much as the larches themselves. And again it occurred to me that the best Lakeland stonework can do that. Someone decreed that these trees were worthy of something special by way of protection: not just an efficient defence against the grazing tribes, but a thing of some elegance in its own right that would complement rather than detract from the elegance of the larches. It is a job very well done. Surely even Wordsworth would have approved.

The middle ground was a wedge of slate-grey lake, Ullswater at its edgiest, flecked with white where the wind drove the massed ranks of ripples and waves in long diagonal parallels that thumped and splintered and collapsed against the shoreline rocks. In the middle of that portion of lake that was not concealed either by the lie of the land or the tumbledown of the sky and its processional showers, the troubled water seethed around a tiny island, so tiny that the maps don't trouble to name it. So tiny that it is scarcely wider than the outward reach of two Scots pines that grow there. There may just be room for a third tree on the island, there is certainly no room for a fourth. The setting is so exposed that not even juniper has attempted a toehold there. The two pines appear to be thriving, though, one half as big again as the other in height, girth and volume. In recognition of the severity of the regime they must thole, the acutely exposed nature of their place on the map, the two trees reach for each other. The longest limb of the larger tree is a horizontally extended arm, a protective gesture that almost touches the trunk of the smaller tree, which in turn arches its upper trunk towards its protector. It is tempting to conclude that nature cut them a raw deal when the berths were being handed out, yet they dug in and appear to be making the most of it: they are free from the attentions of the grazing tribes, they are never going to run out of water and the lake is well sheltered from prevailing winds. So perhaps their situation is more favourable than it might appear at first glance, and short of a particularly unlucky lightning strike, their days look well starred. I know a good Scots pine when I see one, and I think of these two islanders as among the most appealing ambassadors of wild beauty in all Lakeland.

The hour reduced down to a handful of elementals. The trees and rocks where I sat slowly established in me a sense of tranquillity, of sanctuary, a response to the febrile nature of the airspace beyond: the pervasive, hoarse chant of winds, the almost total obliteration of the far shore and its mountains. I was aware of the storm, I had a window seat from which to admire the storm, but I was not *of* the storm.

That handful of square yards of shelter I chanced upon little more than an hour ago felt curiously familiar, as if I had been here before. Or was it simply the situation I was familiar with? Did I slip into a kind of fellow feeling for that here-and-now because I know so well comparable moments and sanctuaries among the eagle mountains of home? Did I recognise the same sense of gratitude at the stance of two trees and their relationship with each other and the rocks to which they were wedded for life…recognised and acknowledged their worth on such a Lakeland day? I remembered something Emerson wrote in "Nature", the better part of 200 years ago, and scribbled its essence into a notebook so that I might tidy it up into his actual words that evening:

…a decorum and sanctity reign…I am nothing. I see all. The waving of the boughs in the storm, is new to me and old. It takes me by surprise, and yet is not unknown…It is certain that the power to produce this delight does not reside in nature, but in man, or in a harmony of both. It is necessary to use these pleasures with great temperance. For nature is

not always tricked in holiday attire, but the same scene which yesterday breathed perfume and glittered...is overspread with melancholy today...

I wrote down a kind of inventory of the moment, and headed it with the phrase of Emerson's that I did recall correctly: "I am nothing. I see all." Because at that moment it encapsulated exactly my approach to the job in hand, to the distillation of that landscape in that mood, "overspread with melancholy". Become landscape by becoming nothing, nothing but a pair of seeing eyes.

There was something appropriately salutary, too, in the discovery that a way of reaching out to nature which I have long considered my own was being espoused 3,000 miles and almost 200 years away: salutary, but also reassuring, because so much that had lured me to Lakeland, and consumed my time there on a daily basis, had flowed from Emerson in the first place. Or rather the third place after Burns and Wordsworth, but he gave it the voice that would ultimately feed it into my own lifetime, my own landscapes.

So I made my inventory of all that I could see: rock, tree, downhill mountainside that began at my feet, high stone wall, larch wood, grey and white wedge of lake, tiny island with two trees, drawn curtains of cloud and rain. I became all of them, or rather the sum of all of them. I am nothing. I see all. The unwritten subtext of the Emerson passage was that the quality of the seeing intensifies the more you can submerge your awareness of self.

Then out of the greyness that robed the far shore, a small dark shape hardened and advanced. An hour ago, I might not have seen it. But that hour had been spent becoming nothing. Now I *could* see all. The shape was low to the surface of the water and exactly the same palette of greys. It flew on heavy, wide, down-curved, slow-beating wings that did not rise above the horizontal, crossing the wind at an angle, tacking like a well-handled boat. A heron. First thought: why cross the lake in that weather? Why not work the shallows and the shelter of the shore? When I tried to answer my own questions, the best I could come up with was: because it knows what it's doing. Herons are straight-line fliers, more often than not. As-the-heron-flies is much more undeviating than as-the-crow-flies. I put that thought to good use, and then it became clear that her line of travel from out of the gloom and glaur of the west shore and towards the east shore was shaping towards a very specific destination: the island. As she homed in, she raised her wings high to effect a banking turn into a dangle-legged, long-necked landing on its very southernmost tip. In the very instant before landing, that heron was surely the most undignified scrap of wildness in all Ullswater, simultaneously stretched to every extremity of wing, leg and neck, while the wind tormented its excessive drapery of oversized feathers, so that again in that same heart-in-the-mouth instant, one ill-timed gust would surely bring the manoeuvre to a conclusion at best chaotic and at worst fatal by dumping the hapless creature into the water. But in the next instant she was perched, and in the one after that she was crouched, folded, curved, neatly angled, poised.

It had all looked so random, so hit-or-miss, but it transpired that it had been an exercise in precision. When the heron had transformed its shape, softened its profile, become compact (a relative achievement for a heron) and still, it was so aligned with the island's two tree trunks that they constituted the nearest thing to a windbreak to be found anywhere that day the length and breadth of the lake; a windbreak, that is, from which a predatory fisher-bird might fish.

I reflected on the similarities between her perch and mine. We both had two trees rooted in hard rock for company and shelter, the better to go about our day's work: the heron's to find a meal, mine to write. In addition, we had both relied on an eye for the lie of the land and that had determined our choices of perch. And having perched and adjusted to the surroundings, we required stillness and patience to get the job done. Eventually (I had no idea how long we had held our stillnesses), she slowly assumed a more upright stance until she was vaguely arboreal herself, and on that splinter of an island that she shared with nothing but two trees, her new stance had the curious effect of making her less visible, for now all three of the island's creatures shared planted lives, erect and stoically silhouetted against the water, and only the foliage of the pines and the plumage of the heron were rendered restless by the wind. Then, by degrees, the heron's neck tilted lower and towards the water's edge just inches beyond her feet. No shallows to wade in there, for the steepness of the hillsides on both shores of Ullswater does not stop at the surface of the water; and hereabouts, the depth is anything up to 200 feet, and given the narrowness of the lake, nature leaves little room for manoeuvre for a wading bird, even one that wades on stilts.

The heron tilted forward from the waist (or where the waist would have been if herons possessed a waist), and with a lunge more like a hammer than a spear, lifted a six-inch-long fish from the water, adjusted its grip on the fish from sideways to head first, and swallowed it hole.

"You've done that before," I mouthed silently. Clearly the tail of the island is a regular beat for a working heron, and with good reason.

Down out of the murky north, a black shape, a low-slung flying cross, diced with wind and wavetops. This was no heron. For a start, it landed on the water. For perhaps a minute it came and went with every crest and trough of every wave. The cormorant is immune to storm. A memory gatecrashed my vigil, the tail of a hurricane swiping the lighthouse and the rocks of Briaghlann at Ardnamurchan Point thirty years before. At noon the sky had fallen on the ocean as black as night, an end-of-the-world shade; gusts that made standing upright difficult sliced lumps off the crests of waves the size of headlands. Ullswater was hardly that, but what triggered the memory, bridged the decades and united the two encounters was cormorants. At the height of that old storm I had glimpsed two cormorants riding that hugely corrugated ocean. No point in flying over such a sea, so sit on it. And now on Ullswater, a downwind cormorant that looked as if it might be having trouble staying ahead of the wind took a similar kind of evasive action and sat on the waves. The cormorant also knows what the heron does not, that a storm on the water, whether inland lake or open ocean, is only a storm at the surface. The depths remain tranquil.

When it dived, the cormorant launched itself upwards apparently from its tail, cleared the surface in a shallow black curve, the tail barely out of the water before the head immersed and the whole straightening body followed it down into those tranquil depths. There are few sights that more readily set a Lakeland fisherman's teeth on edge than an Ullswater cormorant going under, not least because it is an infinitely more skilled fisher than any mere human, and because its preferred quarry hereabouts is a Lakeland specialist: schelly.

I don't fish. I never fished. The schelly was never on my radar, and my ignorance would surely have remained intact had I not mentioned that I was writing this book centred around Ullswater to my Stirling GP, Dr Ian Hanley, at which point the conversation shifted from the minor ailment it had begun with to his impressive knowledge of the schelly, its specific haunts and the exclusive nature of its presence here. From that five-minute conversation I literally went to work on the subject. Back in Lakeland, I looked out for cormorants.

The schelly is a small whitefish. The record catch is 2lbs ½oz. We're not talking *The Old Man and the Sea* here. Just to be clear then: I don't give a damn if I see a cormorant scoff a schelly. Firstly, the chances are that I wouldn't recognise the fish as a schelly anyway, and secondly, I don't fish. But what interested me about it in particular is that it is an Ice Age throwback and its only habitat is one of four Lakeland watersheets: Ullswater, Haweswater, Red Tarn under Catstye Cam, and Angle Tarn to the south of Angletarn Pikes, which in turn are to the south of Place Fell.

Schellies also like the depths of their watersheets rather than the surface, which takes them out of the range of herons and ospreys, for example, but it puts them on the wrong end of what it is that cormorants do best. I am guessing that cormorants don't spend too much time – if any at all – mountaineering up at Red Tarn and Angle Tarn. It is simply not in the nature of the beast. The schelly appears to thrive there. Cormorants are plentiful enough around Ullswater, although not so plentiful that they trouble the stability of the schelly population, but Haweswater is a different kettle of fish, for there it has been deemed necessary to kill cormorants. The official terminology is "cull", but it is killing, whatever you call it. Someone points a rifle, pulls a trigger, a cormorant dies. The theory is that because Haweswater's role as a reservoir requires "abstraction" of water, it makes schellies easier to catch if you are a cormorant, leaving too few for fishermen to catch without threatening the schelly population. But the suspect conclusion drawn by whomsoever comes to such conclusions is that cormorants are destabilising that population, and therefore they must be killed. This ignores two factors that fall into the category of the bleeding obvious to the rest of us. One is that when the water level is low due to the abstractions, wild weather is apt to throw schellies on to the shore, where they turn up dead, a toll taken not by cormorant but rather, however inadvertently, by United Utilities. The other is that conditions in the original pre-1937 Mardale Valley lake (the one left behind, like the other three schelly watersheets, by retreating glaciers) were more or less devastated by the decision to build a dam and raise the water level of Haweswater by ninety-five feet and subject it to drastic fluctuations. If you want to know how to destabilise the natural community that inhabits any body of water, there is the perfect recipe.

If all that seems like an undue fuss to make about a fish, consider this. It is a curiosity of our species and our age that whenever we interfere with natural processes only to discover that some of the consequences of our actions are inconvenient for us, we point the finger at nature instead of looking for the culprit in the mirror, which is where it can invariably be found.

Schellies and cormorants co-existed well enough for thousands of years at the original Haweswater, the one designed by nature. Problems arose after it was redesigned by people trying to solve the problems of Manchester's insatiable thirst for water. It is all a symptom of the same attitudes that pervade grouse moor estates, deer forest estates, drained wetlands, hill sheep farms, deforestation, over-fishing, over-intensified farming, all monocultures. The same attitudes breed hostility to the idea of reintroducing species we have wiped out, and indifference to the ones we are in the throes of wiping out. There is an essential principle of nature at work in all this. It is that the number of predators is directly related to availability of prey species. There is no such thing as too many predators in nature because there cannot be an abundance of predators without a superabundance of prey. It is simply not possible.

Killing cormorants because they may or may not be killing schellies should not happen in a national park. The rationale should form no part of national park philosophy. Killing natural predators – any predators – because our species has a vested interest in what they may or may not kill should be unacceptable in any landscape. In a national park, and especially in *this* national park, it is simply unworthy behaviour. In *this* national park because as one of the very first national parks in Britain, whose possible birth was hinted at by Wordsworth and only became reality because, as we have seen, the great and the good of American nature conservation gave the national park concept life having nurtured that Wordsworthian seed. *This* national park has a duty to set the example for the rest to follow. Nature should be its overriding priority, and it is as simple as that.

★ ★ ★

Back on Ullswater, I had seen in my binoculars from two or three hundred yards away an Ullswater cormorant dive from a sitting start on the surface of the water. Perhaps half a minute later, it surfaced to the south of the island with a fish. I have no idea what kind of fish, any more than I know what fish the heron had caught. But, like the heron, it transferred the fish from sideways in its bill to lengthways and head-first. Then it swallowed. Then it flew low and slow to the island, and, like the heron, landed there into the wind. It perched at the other end of the island from the heron, which made no acknowledgement of its arrival. I wondered if they knew each other, like the robin and the wren on the barn roof.

The weather worsened. The wind strengthened. The rain intensified, slewed across the lake in thick diagonals. It made the binoculars more or less useless. Visibility blurred.

I decided to move downhill to the larch wood. My last view of the island, and without the binoculars, suggested it was home to two pine trees and two unidentifiable, stunted and deformed trees, one at each end. Neither of these tree shapes looked like a bird. But they stood tall and slim and bore with stoic stillness the worst the storm could throw at them, and in that regard they were as timeless as the pines.

Seven

A Sense of Place Fell

"I have been in the hills all day;
"I have not heard the news."
No, but you heard instead
The mountain mosses singing at your tread,
And saw the views
Heart-lifting, of the shadows in the bay.
Down, down and down below
You looked to where men count the days;
But here, where winter stays
And sudden drops his cloak and turns to spring
Is no such thing.
Here is the open heaven, spinning and standing fast,
Held on the big tops' shoulders; here is height
Soaring beyond mortality; and air
That moves eternal there
Which but to taste, teaches delight
And heals time past.

> Extract from "Levavi oculos", by Marion
> Campbell, from her book *Argyll – The Enduring*
> *Heartland* (Turnstone Books, 1977)

THIS SEARCH FOR MY IDEA of wildness in Lakeland was
always destined to linger off-piste, along scrambly hillsides, by woods high- and low-lying, by watersheets and

waterfalls, becks and backwaters, those covert byways where nature also lingers and uses wildness to tailor the land… all of these in preference to the summits and high ridges of the fells and the beaten paths that lead to them, not to mention the ever-increasing volume (in both numbers and decibels) of the path-beaters themselves. But one summit recommended itself above all the others as soon as Ullswater settled into place in my mind as a kind of fulcrum, the still centre of the enterprise. The shape of Ullswater is such that it is forever hiding long views of its mountain walls from itself, and vice versa. Curiously enough, when I went in search of a sense of place that the byways and backwaters could not offer, it was a mountain called Place that pro-vided the solution. Place Fell is a bizarre name even by the standards of Lakeland fells, but it served my purpose because it lies in the crook of Ullswater's elbow. As Lakeland summits go, it is relatively unsung. But the more I looked at it, the more I traversed and scrambled about its eastern slopes above the lake, the more I wandered that shore, the more I admired the mountain slopes and summits above Glenridding, Grisedale, Deepdale and Dovedale and the crag-girt fells above Kirkstone Pass (these seemed to me to represent this book's southern frontier, as Bowscale did its northern one), the more I thought that Place Fell alone offered a unique perspective.

I chose October, the oaks beginning to turn, bracken and heather smoored in rust. Every time I walked up through oak woods here, I admired the many-textured, multi-coloured cloak they cast about the lower slopes, their scattered copses tied together by the vivid, porpoising flight and theatrical cackles of green woodpeckers. The first of them that morning cast off from a larch 200 yards away and came lolloping through the air fifty feet above the slope, chuckling to itself at some donnish woodpecker joke it had just heard back in the larches. When it reached the oaks it bypassed the first few trees and chose to perch (upright as always, how do they *do* that?) on the trunk nearest to where I stood. Almost at once, it seemed suddenly to notice me there in a small clearing, binoculars raised. Very slowly, it began to side-step its way round the trunk (still vertical), a method of locomotion that struck me as vaguely creepy. It is a curiosity of such a blatant bird (green and grey and black and bright red and blazing yellow and that far-carrying, glass-shattering call), that it "hides" when it knows it's been spotted. It was as though it thought that if it moved sideways very, very slowly round to the other side of the tree it would be safe, instead of which, my attention and raised binoculars were riveted. After a few seconds it had disappeared. I waited to see if it would re-emerge or fly off, but after five minutes it had done neither.

Silence.

I imagined it having front-pointed up the far side of the trunk until it reached the angle of the first limb where its huge feet had cramponed into the bark and its rigid tail feathers belayed each move. Three points of contact at all times.

What would happen if I inched round the tree the other way, keeping a few yards away from the trunk? Sidestepping in silence like a woodpecker – admittedly, a six-foot-tall, thirteen-and-a-half-stone woodpecker, but wearing woodland-shaded clothes, only the green and black of him (no red, no yellow) – I started circling, continued until I had covered 180 degrees. The far side of the tree was completely devoid of green woodpeckers.

I considered the possibilities. One – it had climbed right up the blind side of the tree into the canopy and lit out from there into the mountain air (unlikely, surely I would have seen it fly). Two – it had cramponed backwards down the trunk to the ground and walked away across the woodland floor until it judged itself safe to fly (equally unlikely, I have never heard of such a thing among birds of any of the tribes of this country). Or three – and as I edged back round the way I had come to where the woodpecker had originally perched, there it was, back in the same place. It began at once, to retrace its sideways steps back round the tree again, this time in the opposite direction. This, I thought, could go on for long enough. It was clearly discomfited by my presence. The considerate thing to do was to remove myself from the situation. I walked away uphill, through the trees and onto the mountain path, at which point I heard a high-decibel giggle, and then I too was laughing.

Across the lake, more oak woods thickened around the ends of the long shoulders and buttresses delineating the valleys that pour down out of the black folds and shadows of Helvellyn and Fairfield, black because the sun stood behind them. The sky there was festive with pale and black and blazing white-gold clouds. Shredding winds raced in among them. Sunlight flared and dowsed, and the land in the valleys brightened and darkened; it laved the bright throat of Deepdale, even as cloud shadow surged down through Grisedale as if a glacier still flowed there, the one startling green, the other dark and smoky grey and bluish black. The transformations were many and fleeting, restless and hypnotic. The land itself was as animated as the sky. The shadows and sheen of clouds and beams flew across mountain flanks and valley floors. The higher I climbed, the wider the sorcerer's canvas. But south over Kirkstone Pass the mountain shapes blurred and receded among thickening masses of rain clouds on a mission. It would be the sky, then, that shaped and shaded the day and burned it indelibly into the memory. By the time I reached my chosen summit, it had become the centerpiece of a three-way contest involving two weather systems and irrepressible sunlight.

I could see now that the two valleys – Deepdale and Grisedale, the sunlit and the shadowed – all but encircled a squat and bulky mountain. It rose from the wider, flat-bottomed valley south of Patterdale in three distinct phases, each a swelling curve with a gently flattened top. The movement of sunlight and shadow across its contours suggested head and sloping shoulders, well-rounded belly and folded knees. For the first time, I saw St Sunday Crag in the guise of a seated Buddha, and I have never quite been able to shake off the image since that day. I follow no religion, but if I ever did, a Buddha enthroned among mountains with his head nudging clouds flamed by sun and shredded by wind, summoning the elements to burnish his omnipotence...I imagine I could do a lot worse. If memory serves from a teenage Church of Scotland Bible class lesson in Dundee discussing other religions, Buddha was still plain Siddhartha when he spent a fateful night in deep meditation under the

Bodhi Tree, resolving to stay there until he uncovered the elusive truths that would provide him with the key to end all the world's suffering. What happened that night afforded him the knowledge he lacked, a vision of everything in the universe, a knowledge that in time would evolve into the essential tenets of Buddhism.

Like many defining moments among the world's religions, it is, at the very least, a good story. But in the tumultuous 21st-century conditions of that Lakeland corner as seen from high on Place Fell that day, it was easy to be moved in a vaguely apostolic way by the ample girth of St Sunday Crag preaching eternal truths in a trance of profound understanding. For me, it is nature, the land itself that dispenses eternal universal truths, and whenever it stops me in my tracks, my discipleship insists that the least I can do is listen. And when I do stop and listen, I try and make a space in the day, find a tree or a rock for my back, and sit and open my mind to what the land has to say. Do not imagine for one moment that I lay claim to grotesque illusions of deity – as far from that as is humanly possible – but the reason why I warmed to that seated Buddha image for St Sunday Crag is because the stillness of landscape is always (and however fleetingly it may be achieved) what the nature writer in me strives for, and the point at which I part company with the mountaineers whose mission is to reach the summit so that they might pronounce it climbed and tick it off on a list.

In Scotland, the obsession is Munro-bagging; in Lakeland, it's the Wainwrights; to the far-travelled it's the Seven Summits (the high point of each continent); and to the mountaineering superstars it's the world's fourteen 8,000-metre peaks, which one Nepalese mountaineer climbed in an improbable record time of six months. The only certainty to evolve from that kind of relationship with mountains is that one day someone will do it in five. The point is that turning mountains, of all things, into collectibles – compiling them into tickable lists – strikes me as a disappointing response in a human breast. As I understand it, to qualify as a "Wainwright", the mountain must simply appear as a named fell in his series of seven Lakeland guides. I don't know, because I never met the man, but I imagine the idea horrified him. Hill-going traditions are essentially local, and therefore idiosyncratic, and to the outsider the rationale is very often elusive. On that basis, I find the Wainwrights concept elusive. But, then, I think Munro-bagging is nuts. The original 3,000-foot cut-off point, the arbitrary qualification on the list compiled by Sir Hugh Munro, was bizarre enough. But no hill-walking map now posts heights in feet, but rather in metres. So the Munro-bagging sheep who still flock to the concept and become "Munroists", with a certificate to prove it, have climbed every mountain over 914.4 metres. As things stand, there are 282 Munros, but it was not always thus. At one point in my climbing life there were only 278, but more sophisticated measuring equipment has elevated some and demoted others. So if your certificate was issued when there were only 278, and you subsequently became unfit to climb, strictly speaking you should be delisted too, but it doesn't work that way. At least I don't think it works that way.

Rational-thinking human beings from furth of Lakeland

were always going to have trouble with the phenomenon that is the Bob Graham Round. Graham was a fell runner who once ran over forty-two Lakeland summits in twenty-four hours. Why? Nobody knows. Except perhaps to show that he could. You can now *walk* the Bob Graham Round in a guided walking holiday over six or seven days and pay quite a few hundred pounds for the privilege. One tour company calls it "strenuous", and for most people it is. Graham, one imagines, would argue that forty-two in twenty-four hours was strenuous and that the walking round named in his honour is a hands-in-pooches stroll in the park. The company's website lists among the highlights "the sense of achievement having successfully conquered this challenging Lake District walk".

Conquered? Talk about elusive.

I climbed quite hard in my twenties and thirties, without ever making lists of what I climbed. I fell away from the handful of others with whom I climbed because I kept wanting to go back to the same handful of summits again and again, the ones that magnetised my gaze and spoke to me of…and that's where my philosophy runs out of words. But the ones to which I felt a connection. Then I started to watch golden eagles and that changed everything. I was asked to help in a watch on a golden eagle eyrie that had been targeted by egg thieves for seven consecutive years. I got hooked on simply seeing eagles so often. But after the first two years, I started to get curious about what the eagles were doing when they were away from their nest crag, when they were out in their territory. And slowly, over years, I got to know the eagles' territory, and started to see how eagles worked for their living and, as I travelled around Scotland, how that changed from bird to bird, pair to pair, mainland to island. In the process, I also began to encounter their neighbours, their fellow travellers, their prey species and the ones they left alone, and my mountain days and my whole life changed utterly and forever. I became a nature writer, and in pursuit of that ideal, I quickly learned that stillness was as important as travel, and that becoming a part of the landscape was infinitely more important than climbing to the top of it. As much as anything, Place Fell was to be my eagle's eye-view of the land with which I was seeking to make some kind of accommodation. The summit was a surprise, a low rocky ridge with a hefty cairn and a scattering of tiny tarns. It rained into my coffee, but it was a light and wind-borne rain, more chilling than wettening.

Meanwhile, storm clouds descended mob-handed on Kirkstone Pass. Its mountains blackened and vanished, weighted down by the sheer force of angry rains. Yet high above the storm the clouds were vivid white and scintillating gold, for there, above about 4,000 feet, sunlight still held sway, still rose and fell, and appeared to drag clouds with it. These high-speed collisions of contrary weathers spread all across the sky. Their effect was no more alluring than on Hartsop above How, the ridge that holds Deepdale in place to the south, where, against the blue-black background wall of Hart Crag, the ridge began to smoulder like a craterless volcano. Some trick of the wind was at work in Dovedale on the far side of the ridge, pushing cloud deep down into the valley then hurling it against mountain walls so that it surged up the face. Where it met the ridge it caught the sunlight and burst apart in the same instant, so that it was both white fire and white smoke that spread along the ridge and flung vertically twisting columns into the air, heightening the illusion of a living creature with antennae and hell-bent on the heights of Hart Crag and Fairfield.

In all that mountainous company, what wasn't bluish black was out-and-out black. Above the summits, storm clouds hurried down in breaking black waves, but there too the wind shredded them and sunlight burst in on the shreds, rimming the black with gold, and the topmost heights were alive with streamers of white that constantly tore apart and reformed, a wild chaos of writhing shapelessness. Raw energy in its simplest, purest form.

The down-thrusting sky had obliterated Kirkstone Pass and all its mountains. And then it curved, and then it swirled back north, so that suddenly Place Fell, which had offered a window on the storm, was now directly in its path. Watching the frontier of storm home in on the very rock where you stand is one of mountaineering's more humbling moments. It appeared to follow the very path by which you climbed, as if it were a hound following your spoor, as if it sought you out. It came on, climbing at pace, and it was two-toned – pale grey and fragmented where it jigged and reeled among the hill rocks and grasses, leaden and solid above. Never was a fusion of greys so compelling. It swallowed Angletarn Pikes whole. Unseen beyond them, the tarn must have galvanised with sudden surges of white water, miniature whirlwinds, and with all its wildfowl stashed away behind the headland that guards and shelters a small bay from which a giddy beck slaloms down the short, sharp shock of its watercourse and clatters gleefully into the valley of Goldrill Beck, far, far below. But then, having made whatever point nature had in mind for you, it swerved again and drove away from Place Fell, dragging its colossal two-toned bulk eastwards, and in the process it devoured High Street and set about tormenting the creatures – human and otherwise – around Haweswater and beyond.

Peering south from Place Fell into the fraying underbelly of the departing storm, there was a sudden flash of bright green and a hard-edged sheet of something like polished jet beyond – a triangular wedge of flat fields caught up in the dance of a stray beam of sunlight, and the unruffled refuge of Brothers Water, moodily reflecting every shade of mountain black and storm cloud grey.

★ ★ ★

The storm released its stranglehold. Cloud climbed and frayed away as if it had never been, which, sooner or later, is what clouds do. Wind dwindled, air sweetened, land sighed.

I came away contented. This is my way with mountains now. I take them one at a time. I may or may not go to the top. I subscribe to no one's list of mountains.

I treasure the mountain's company. I linger there. I watch. I photograph, draw, write it down (or at least some facet of it, what sets it apart from all other mountains, for they all have something). I watch its birds, its animals, its flowers, its trees. All that takes time. But I take time. The mountain, after all, is quite possibly the oldest thing you have ever seen, hundreds if not thousands of millions of years old.

The only thing you will ever meet that is older is another mountain. The mountain is made of time. The least I can do is take the necessary time to pay my respects.

It occurred to me at the end of my Place Fell day that if I had signed up instead for a week-long guided tour of the Bob Graham Round, on the longest day of that mountaineering week I would have been expected to cover twenty miles and the summits of fifteen fells with a total ascent of over 7,000 feet. But I spent a single day on Place Fell and its landscape setting, one fell, a total ascent of just over 2,000 feet. And what it comes down to is this: do you want to climb the mountain or do you want to know the mountain? In the back of my mind, whenever my thoughts tend this way, is an entry in the visitors' book in a bothy under wondrous An Teallach in the West Highlands. It read: "F★★★ the Munros, I'm going to climb An Teallach 280 times." I would like to have bought the writer a drink.

You can climb the mountain, touch the cairn, pronounce it climbed, put a tick against its name on someone else's list, turn your back on it and go on to the next one, and that is one way to approach the mountain. But there is the mountain, and there is the beauty of the mountain. There is climbing the mountain and there is breathing the mountain in, and in stillness there is listening to the mountain, and in the breathing in and the listening…there lies the buried treasure that is the wildness of the mountain.

Eight

Golden Eagle, Silver Swan

ANGLE TARN LIES HIGH AND ALONE in a spacious arc of hills, wind-washed, bone-bare, tree-starved. Notwithstanding the tree-starvation, I would have liked it anyway, just for itself and where it lies and how it looks and how you come upon it from below so that it's unseen until the last moment and its suddenness and its brightness startles you when you get there. All that is regardless of the golden eagle, regardless of the swans, regardless of the red deer, regardless of the wild-fowl, regardless of the dazzling, shining arc of a leaping fish. It is one of those enigmas-in-landscape that linger stub-bornly in my mind when I am hundreds of miles away from Lakeland, which after all is most of the time. Sometimes I think about what happens there all the hours of all the days and nights of my being somewhere else. There are other lonelier and arguably lovelier Lakeland tarns, swaddled in the lap of huge cliffs or towered over by mountain super-stars. But these never trouble my far-off thoughts in the way that Angle Tarn does. Angle Tarn rather got under my skin.

The swans had a lot to do with it, for I am addictive haunter of swan-waters in my own land, and the addiction travels effortlessly with me in lands other than my own. I still think of a trumpeter swan family on a small lake far up the valley of the Yukon, somewhere near the Canada/ Alaska border – giants of the swan race with a ten-foot wingspan, their lake girdled by beaver woods and beaver dams and beaver lodges and beaver-sculpted wetland – and that was more than twenty years ago now. A whooper swan pair building a nest built on the edge of black volcanic sand in Iceland with an unrestricted view of Hecla, Icelandic volcano of distinction, and that was nearer thirty years ago. And just three years ago, a whooper swan family with six cygnets on a lake in the thrall of an exquisite mountain in Arctic Norway's Lofoten Islands (see *The Nature of Summer*, Saraband, 2020). I think of these again and again, although I only ever saw each of them once. Such is my thraldom for the tribe of wild swans. The passage of time does not diminish the clarity of their memory. At the root of this swan addiction are two watersheets that I got to know around the same time, and in the years immediately before I abandoned my life as a newspaper journalist in 1988 to fashion a life out of writing about nature. One is a farm pond in West Lothian, a dozen miles west of Edinburgh. The other is Loch Lubnaig, near the eastern edge of the Loch Lomond and the Trossachs National Park.

The farm pond has a man-made island where mute swans nest, shaded by a willow tree. I got to know Brian Cadzow, the farmer who built the island by sledging rocks out across midwinter ice. He also planted the tree and arranged for an annual bale of straw to be deposited on it every February, building materials for the swans. They had previously nested on the shore, but fell victim too often to foxes. They took to the island at once and regularly fledged seven cygnets, aided by handouts of food from the Cadzows. The project was a huge contribution to the wellbeing of mute swans in central Scotland. Brian Cadzow died on my birthday in

1994. The fields around the pond have since been covered in new houses. Swan life endures on the pond.

Loch Lubnaig was the scene for the most ambitious wildlife project I ever undertook, a study of a pair of mute swans that nested in a reedbed at the north end of the loch. I watched them over thirty years, and they figure in my three swan books and in countless newspaper and magazine articles and a series of radio programmes. They broke all the rules all the time, they lived long lives (the huge cob at least thirty years, his mate at least twenty-five) and I became a part of their landscape as they became a part of mine. The project ended when the swans died, within three years of each other. But the loch is still central to my nature-writing life and every year I stop to watch today's resident pair, to remember, and to compare notes. The nest site is as thrawn as ever, life for mute swans no less difficult. Yet their loyalty to it is unswerving. Every winter, whooper swans on their migratory travels touch down for a few hours, a few days, a few weeks.

Angle Tarn is not typical mute swan nesting territory and I doubt if they have ever nested there, but I stumbled on what I imagine can only ever be an occasional visitation. They would have climbed up from Brothers Water, a little to the south of where Angle Tarn Beck tumbles into Goldrill Beck in the valley far below. I would love to see them make that ascent, for within enclosed mountain valleys, swans climb in circuits using the full width of the valley, each circuit gaining height on the one before, until finally they level out and clear the watershed, the summit, the ridge, or whatever obstacle is in their way. The flight of swans, especially protracted flight, marries one of the most beautiful sights in all nature in these islands with rhythmic and relentless power. With mute swans, the rhythm is enhanced by its far-carrying wing-song: its pitch suggests the sound of a child's humming top being constantly interrupted. Unmated birds routinely cross the North Sea from mainland Europe for the winter, often flying at wave-top level. Sometimes they will put down on the sea for a few hours of darkness, or resume when the moon rises. Imagine it: a skein of swans flying over the open sea by moonlight.

So it thrilled me to find a pair of mute swans on what was only my second visit to Angle Tarn. They were resting on the water in sunlight, heads sunk deep in the feathers of their backs and folded wings and facing their tails, doing nothing at all other than recovering their composure having just climbed up from Brothers Water through tiers of rocking winds. The water was relatively calm in the sheltered bay where they sat, but out in the middle of the tarn it was kicking up into sharp-edged crests edged in white, and in that sunlight those crests were royal blue and shading to navy in their own shadows. At first glance, you might say that the swans were simply a blaze of white. But the painter C.F. Tunnicliffe taught me otherwise years ago when I read *Bird Portraiture* (The Studio, 1945). In the text to accompany a painting of swans, he dismissed the idea of a purely "white" bird, for his artist's eyes knew those properties in swan feathers that accommodate the shade and tone and colour of their immediate surroundings in pale infusions. For example:

Golden Eagle, Silver Swan

Notice the yellow tinge in the feathers of neck and upper breast, and the cold bluish purity of the back, wings and tail. Note also the colour of the shadowed under-surfaces and how it is influenced by the colour of the ground on which he is standing: if he is standing on green grass, then the under-parts reflect a greenish colour, whereas if he were on dry, golden sand, the reflected colour would be of a distinctly warm tint; or again, if he were flying over water, his breast, belly and under-wings would take on a colder tint, especially if the water were reflecting a blue or grey sky.

Water or snow changes everything. Only the upper surfaces of a swimming swan are lit by sunlight…

…the rest of him being in shadow and appearing dark violet against the bright water; in fact, but for the light on his back and the top of his head he appears as a dark silhouette in relation to the high tone of the water…

A swan in snow can look anything but white:

…Now you can see how yellow his neck is, and, to a lesser extent, the rest of his upper plumage. Note also the reflected snow light on his undersides which makes them look almost the same tone as, or even lighter than, his top surfaces…

Over the thirty-something years I have been a nature writer for a living, I have found that the more I consult artists and keep their company, the more I learn from the way they see, the better I see too; and the more nature reveals of itself, the more there is to find, the more complete my understanding of a single creature becomes.

The Angle Tarn cob stepped up from floating on the surface to stand on a submerged rock, a typical pose for swans everywhere. Just as they like to feed through shallow water, they often preen on a submerged rock so that only their feet and an inch or two of legs are underwater. In such circumstances, there seems to be an element of comfort in direct contact with open water, perhaps because it offers a quick retreat from danger, for swans are more likely to put distance between themselves and danger by swimming away from it, and flight is a last resort. In mountains where valleys limit their flight options, it is noticeable that they climb and descend over water whenever possible. They are extremely accomplished at forced landings. When they nest, the territory they defend is a piece of water, not the airspace above it.

As soon as the cob began to preen, its subtle palette became more obvious in response to the constant movement of neck and head and plumage. With the swan standing side-on and the beak working through the feathers of the far wing, its head and upper neck were immediately much more obviously yellow than the wing. And by curving and angling the neck away from its breast, a shadow appeared at the base of the neck that was a deep shade of blue-grey, with a subtle hint of mauve. The shadow was a perfect triangle shape except that the outer edge was almost imperceptibly curved. And it was paler at the bottom than the top. I could not remember ever seeing that shadow before. A paler blue-grey delineated the upper edge of the nearer wing where it lay neatly folded, as yet undisturbed by the preening process. The delineation lay in two narrow strips, one almost horizontal at the top but with a slight down-curve at the end that paled as it curved; the other curved more steeply down towards the tail, and was paler and greyer. A third strip below the second, but darker blue-grey than the others, seemed to spring from lower on the wing, a single wind-nudged feather that produced its own darker shadow. From both upper strips, parallel furrows in pale echoes of the same shade spilled diagonally down the wing. The base of the tail was one more variation of the blue-grey theme, a broad band of it, yet the tip of the tail was unblemished white. From stem to stern of the swan's "hull", the undersides were in shadow, darkly so – almost black – at the breast, and paling all the way back towards the tail. Hints of yellow from bounced sunlight and blue from the water beneath were flecked throughout the long under-curve of the standing swan and all the way back to the tail. Finally, as a kind of miraculous footnote, the whole was caught and brightened in the tarn's reflection and liberally stippled with royal blue, and there that fugitive yellow shade was much more pronounced. So that's why Mr Tunnicliffe would have you know that there is no such thing as a white swan.

Sometimes watching a swan feels like watching a blank canvas that nature simply goes to work on, altering its approach to familiar themes and shapes every time, like Cézanne and his endless series of paintings of Mont Sainte-Victoire that got more and more abstract as the years passed and he experimented ever more boldly with the first building blocks of cubism.

The pen had been all but motionless, but she suddenly stirred. Her neck, which had been draped in a fluent curve along her back, was suddenly erect, a movement that immediately threw a pale blue shadow along her back. The gesture disturbed the cob in mid-preen, and his neck also uncoiled and straightened, head held high like his mate; given his higher stance and greater bulk, he towered over her. Their attention was suddenly focused on the northern sky. They muttered to each other, softly grunted syllables, then at the upper limit of my hearing and some seconds before I could see anything at all, I heard the unmistakable voices of whooper swans.

They appeared to the west of Angletarn Pikes, so that I wondered if they were following the trough of Ullswater, Goldrill Beck and the beckoning crest of Kirkstone Pass, for I had often seen whoopers follow similar sequences of landmarks on migration wanderings through Scotland. These were far higher than the tarn and apparently making steadily south, but decades of watching swans in wild lands have persuaded me that the one thing most likely to lure swans in flight down onto a particular watersheet is the presence of other swans there. The sun was on them in a way that it was not on the tarn swans, and the light that it shed momentarily coated them in brilliant silver as they changed course and headed towards Angle Tarn. They flew the entire length of the tarn from north to south and then at its far end they began abruptly to lose height in a fashion quite unlike anything I had ever seen in mute swans: they pivoted forward so that heads and necks pointed at the surface, tail vertically above and pointing at the sky, and in that fashion they dropped in the tightest of spirals, shedding hundreds of feet in corkscrewing seconds, pulling out no more than twenty feet above the water and cruising down to a wide-winged, web-pattering landing. At once they rose to face each other on the surface with wings threshing back and forward in front of them, voices raised in discordant, brassy notes, before they subsided on the water and began to bathe and preen loudly and expansively. Whooper swans always make quite an entrance. But the mutes, tucked into the quiet bay at the north end where Angle Tarn Beck takes its leave of its parent watersheet, paid them not the slightest attention. By the time I left the tarn, the two pairs of swans were still as far apart as ever, yet I was left with the feeling that had it not been for the presence of the mute swans on the tarn, the whoopers would have flown on, but they diverted because that presence indicated that the tarn was a place of shelter, safety or food – any or all of these – and what more does a pair of migrating swans need than that? My guess is that the mutes were back in the valley by nightfall and the whoopers were gone in the dawn.

I thought back to that first questioning look of the pen when she raised her head from her resting doze. It is not the first time I have acquired first-hand evidence of the capacity of swans to hear or otherwise detect the approach of a specific concern to them while it was still out of sight. In particular, I was watching a widely scattered winter flock of around forty whooper swans in a field at home. They were grazing quietly on grass when suddenly every neck in the field shot straight up and voices were raised all across the flock, an area of at least 200 square yards. The problem was in the west. I wondered if there was a fox in the field, but the impression they gave was of something much further off. The voices held a clear edge of anxiety.

Nothing happened for perhaps ten minutes, during which time the swans had relaxed and grown anxious again. Finally, a huge, bruise-coloured cloud spread across the horizon and advanced at speed. Then there was thunder and lightning and finally a storm of hailstones aslant on a powerhouse wind. It lasted for a quarter of an hour. The swans sat it out with their heads and necks raised. They pointed their bright yellow beaks straight into the slant of the storm. When it passed, they preened fussily and called all across the flock, then settled again as if it had never happened. But it became clear during the storm that they had either heard it or knew of its approach while it was still under the horizon, and long before I heard anything at all. The approach of two whooper swans in fair weather up on Angle Tarn is not quite the same class of intrusion, but the same sense of extra-sensory perception of something while it was still beyond human reach made a lasting impression.

* * *

A few years before the day of the swans, it was a golden eagle that first endeared me to Angle Tarn. By that time, the golden eagle population of all England was down to one. For years after the disappearance of its mate, it had acquired almost legendary status in the rarefied world of golden eagle enthusiasts, but it had also become something of a celebrity, drenched by a certain cast of national newspaper journalism in the clothes of anthropomorphism: the eagle was "love-lorn", "heart-broken", "a widower", one of "nature's lonely hearts club", and worse, much, much worse. It was last seen alive in the autumn of 2015 and it was not long before then that my brother Vic and I wandered that way, heading for the tarn at his suggestion. We were almost there when an old familiar shadow darkened a patch of rock a couple of hundred yards away. The shadow-thrower flew twenty feet above. I hardly ever walk anywhere without binoculars, and I confirmed my first suspicion with a clear view in the glasses, and the significance of this encounter for one who has studied Scottish eagles for forty years, one who lives in a land where the golden eagle population is over 500 breeding pairs and rising...this was a moment that gratified. I was caught unawares. It felt quite emotional.

The shadow was a factor. Again and again, watching golden eagles at home, it is often the shadow of a flying eagle that catches my eye, the way it ripples over boulders and tree canopies, or flips up a buttress like a surfacing whale, a shadow of substance, its own creature, possessed of astounding agility. Nothing stops it or causes it to hesitate. It has always had the effect on me of deepening my connection with golden eagles. The shadow is its land-creature, the part of the eagle that never flies, my earth-born companion. And there it was a few hundred yards from Angle Tarn, and the two ideas have been conjoined in my mind ever since. The story of the golden eagle in Lakeland is well documented. This was my only encounter with the species in England, one that lasted about a minute before it slid across the sky towards Bannerdale with its shadow pushing on ahead of it, and I watched it disappear, wondering if that was it, my once and forever meeting.

It proved to be just that.

Anywhere on Earth that has conjured up both silver swan and golden eagle will always stay with me, and I would never need another excuse to go back. So I went. It was towards the end of winter, the low hills that cradle the tarn patched with old snow, a fresh fall on the crest of High Street showing brightly through two gaps between the three tops to the south and west. That wide view as you come on the tarn from the base of the Pikes has the feel of a set-aside place, as if it were a landscape in waiting. It appeared suddenly from a small rise in the ground in a corral of low hills – Buck Crag, Satura Crag, Brock Crags, Ling Crag – and these had the feeling of having jostled each other to make room for the watersheet, a last gesture by the last of the glaciers as it laid down the architecture of the Lakeland we know today before sliding off downhill into oblivion, until the next time planet Earth decides to obliterate humanity's puny reign under a new welter of ice.

Angle Tarn, of all Lakeland's bodies of water, was the one that recalled Thoreau to mind. He was always an original thinker, he was central to the evolution of the American nature-writing tradition, and 175 years after he moved to Walden Pond, he still is. And Thoreau wrote this:

A lake is the landscape's most beautiful and expressive feature. It is Earth's eye; looking into which the beholder measures the depth of his own nature.

Golden Eagle, Silver Swan

Look down on Angle Tarn from high on the Pikes and see its truth, its unblinking scrutiny of the over-world and the sky, its all-seeing wisdom born of its rootedness in the raw stuff of the Earth, direct descendant of glaciers that moulded from that raw stuff the architecture of mountains. After a while, you may find it hard to hold its gaze. It can unnerve, this eye that never closes, never blinks, this eye that knows all there is to know of the slow wheel of the stars across its line of sight or the flight of swan or eagle. You do well to contemplate the possibilities of what this eye has seen in the 10,000 years or so since the veil of ice was lifted from the meniscus and the world we call Lakeland revealed for the first time. So many of Lakeland's tarns are enclosed by mountain walls. The analogy of Earth's eye doesn't work. But Angle Tarn's situation is an open one: its neighbouring hills lean back, make way. It is a water of Lakeland's roof rather than its floor. Skylight floods it. And this was Thoreau's point about Walden Pond.

Nothing so fair, so pure, and at the same time so large, as a lake, perchance, lies on the surface of the Earth. Sky water. It needs no fence. Nations come and go without defiling it. It is a mirror which no stone can crack…a mirror in which all impurity presented to it sinks…which retains no breath that is breathed on it, but sends its own to float as clouds high above its surface, and be reflected in its bosom still…

I suspect Thoreau was delighted with his "Earth's eye" image. I know I would have been had it been mine! Now, consider this small adornment:

Trees next the shore are the slender eyelashes which fringe it,
and the wooded hills and cliffs around it are its overhanging
brows…

What? You think Angle Tarn has never seen trees? You
think that these shores and those two little islands hard by
the east shore never knew willows, rowans, alders, birches,
pines? You think that hills and cliffs around Angle Tarn were
never wooded overhanging brows too? Stand by the outflow of Angle Tarn Beck and meet the gaze of the tarn
and know it for shed tears that lament the demise of the
thousand years of trees that thrived here (see the stunted
relics on the islands and the occasional niche in a cliff
too difficult for the grazing tribes to reach). The beck is
a headlong plunge to the treed world of Goldrill Beck.
Sheep, thousands of years of sheep, have been humankind's
preoccupation in these mountains – despite the visible
effects on every Lakeland fell that point unerringly to a
beleaguered landscape (which, for all its many beauties,
exists today at a biological level far below its full potential).
And it's not just the sheep hereabouts.

Brock Crag's leading edge, seen from the shore of Angle
Tarn that day against the sky, wore a frieze of red deer
hinds. Around twenty heads stared north-east, every head
and every pair of ears was a silhouette pinned to the mountain edge, the ears straining for confirmation of what eyes
and noses would already have told them. Their attention
was absolute, undivided, the focus of every beast. I tried to
establish the object of the herd's focus with binoculars, but
confirmed only that they were looking towards The Nab,

a narrow and steep-sided hill tapering northwards towards Martindale like a compass needle. The Nab is something of an English red deer shrine, home to what claims to be the oldest herd in England and the only pure-bred one. I assumed these deer above Angle Tarn were part of that herd, and that they had just scented, heard or seen more of their own kind, perhaps a posse of stags mooching moodily across the hill flanks as they approached the annual shedding of their antlers, or grazing on the high slopes. Or perhaps their focus was on men with guns. They will know well enough what that means.

I recognised the attitude of the deer very well, for it was the kind of focused stare I have seen Highland and Hebridean red deer giving to a hunting eagle (as well as men with guns). New-born calves are ambitious prey for golden eagles but not beyond them, still less so for a sea eagle, and there are enough eye-witness accounts in the Highlands of a golden eagle or even a pair acting in concert and panicking a hind into running over a cliff, and feeding for days on the consequences. I wondered if it ever occurred to those Lakeland deer from time to time that their sky had been eagle-free for many seasons, or whether they had no concept of that kind of time and simply relied on race-memory to kick in again instantly if and when another golden eagle ever wandered their way and threw down its shadow on the flanks of their home hills, like a gauntlet at calving time. In much the same way, the elks of Yellowstone National Park in the United States had forgotten how to behave like wild elk in the seventy wolfless years before 1995; but in 1995, when wolves were reintroduced, the elk remembered overnight and their behaviour was changed utterly and forever.

★ ★ ★

There are two surprisingly conspicuous words on the O.S. map that covers the quiet back country between Ullswater and Haweswater, two words that overlap the summit ridge of The Nab and Rampsgill Beck, two words that are not a place name or a natural landscape feature. Instead, they amount to a species of 19th-century shorthand that denotes one of the two most unnatural landscape features anywhere in the country. The very sight of them on a map puts my teeth on edge because of what they represent. In well-spaced type several sizes larger than the names of fells and crags and becks and tarns so that you should be in no doubt of its self-importance, it says, *Deer Forest*. Quite apart from being spectacularly oxymoronic (one of the defining characteristics of the "deer forest" concept is the glaring absence of trees), surely the values it enshrines are 150 years out of date. This also applies, incidentally, to its evil twin of Victorian land management, the grouse moor. Quite apart from any other consideration, why should a deer forest be permitted in a 21st-century national park and World Heritage Site?

The Nab has had a troubled history in the matter of access. The estate's website points out that "it is one of Wainwright's Peaks and is featured in Book 2, The Far Eastern Fells". So it is. Let's see what the guru of all things Lakeland had to say about it:

"Keep Out" notices, barricaded gates, and miles of barbed wire must convey the impression even to the dullest-witted walker that there is no welcome here. That impression is correct. Wandering within the boundaries of the deer forest is not encouraged. Permission to visit the area should be sought at the keeper's Bungalow, and, justifiably, may not be granted.

The suspicion that the word "justifiably" was put there with tongue in cheek is irresistible, for he went on:

The author carried out his exploration surreptitiously, and without permission (not caring to risk a refusal)...

There is more in this vein. Wainwright was writing in the 1950s, and while it's true that the barbed wire fences that irked him so much have been gone for a while now, there are still notices, still echoes of those essentially Victorian attitudes that invented the "deer forest" and sought to put walkers in their place, which is preferably somewhere else:

Persons seeking to gain access to The Nab must first seek permission from the Dalemain Estate Office...

So sayeth the estate's website, to which my Scottish blood's first reaction is, "Or what?" It further sayeth:

Although there is now open access to The Nab the area may be closed at times between September and February for deer management purposes and possibly at other times as required.

All of which is another way of saying that there is no open access unless we say so, which is another way of saying there is no open access. Such a state of affairs is not unknown in my own country but we have the advantage of freedom to roam being enshrined in law, so where intimidation is still practised, it usually doesn't work. Mostly, if not always, common sense keeps walkers and shooters apart in Scotland. It's the sound of the guns that does it. They're armed, we aren't. It's persuasive. Meanwhile, for the tolerant, liberal-minded majority who go to the fells and don't carry guns either, and don't shoot deer for the hell of it and don't see why they should have to ask anyone's permission to put one foot in front of another inside a national park, I recommend the pursuit of freedom to roam as a legal strategy.

There is a particular problem in all this for Lakeland. The ethos that underpins The Nab's deer forest is but one symptom of many, and again I acknowledge my outsider status, but my primary concern is the wellbeing of nature and nature doesn't give a damn about borders, whether national or provincial or national park. Or deer forest, for that matter. The Riggindale eagles did not routinely fly round the boundaries of Dalemain Estate to avoid flying over it, or stay inside the boundaries of the national park because they felt safer outside the one and inside the other. For that matter, the red deer don't stay inside the deer forest and they wander freely for miles around without seeking permission from neighbouring landowners. Surely, even the dullest-witted walker, to borrow Wainwright's pointed phrase, is entitled to question the validity of a national park system that permits such self-centred anomalies from private landowners. Why, the dull-witted walker might ask, should anyone at all be entitled to decide who gets to walk where and when, and for that matter, which species of wildlife get to live and which to die, and especially when the less-than-lofty object of the exercise is that rich men with guns might have the place to themselves so that they can kill deer?

Wider consideration of the situation might look at the management of national parks throughout the length and breadth of Britain, take account of their manifest failings to care for landscape and wildlife, usually at the expense of tourism, and conclude that all national parks should be owned by the nation, as they are in almost every other European nation and in America, which invented the idea, or at least was the first to put it into practice. Instead, what we have is land ownership and management by a coalition of the mostly unwilling – private landowners who often live hundreds if not thousands of miles away, public agencies like the Forestry Commission and water boards, and conservation charities. Governments are not slow to inflict compulsory purchase orders on land required for pet development projects: HS2 springs effortlessly to mind. It should not be beyond the reach of their wits to fund national ownership of national parks by the same means. Secondly, I wonder if it is appropriate that an added burden of responsibility ought to rest on the shoulders of the Lake District National Park because it was one of the first of all Britain's national parks, a trail-blazer. Is it so unreasonable to expect the Lake District National Park to set an example for every other national park to follow, and for that matter, to demonstrate to private landowners outwith the national park system, that honouring the needs of landscape and wildlife – the needs of all nature – as a first priority, is compatible with the needs of the native human population, with national parks, and with an infinitely more thoughtful and compassionate tourism industry? As things stand, there is little evidence that the Lake District National Park Authority has any taste for shouldering that responsibility.

If you would like a sample of how far removed the Lake District National Park is from being taken seriously as a competent role model of nature conservation you might like to consider the following, which is still on its website, ironically on its "Learning" page. Its "Wildlife" segment is mostly about red squirrels, but then there is this:

> *The Lake District National Park is also home to other rare wildlife including red deer, the peregrine falcon, Arctic char fish and Britain's only nesting pairs of golden eagles and ospreys.*

When I first encountered the reference, about two years ago now, I emailed the national park authority, explained who I was and what I was doing, then quoted the website post. I was genuinely trying to be helpful. But before I could say that there hadn't been a pair of golden eagles since 2004, when the resident female died, and none at all since 2015, and that there are ospreys in several other English counties, I was told that if I wanted further information about the eagles I should phone the RSPB. There the conversation ended. There are many occasions in which London politicians and London media of various colours routinely regard the words "Britain" and "England" as interchangeable. I didn't expect it in the Lake District National Park. Now I know that the natives have been a little restless over the last few years, but as I write this, Scotland – with its 500-plus pairs of golden eagles and 200-plus pairs of ospreys – is still in Britain. *Phone the RSPB?*

★ ★ ★

Angle Tarn is special. It is the Earth-eye that sees the vanished trees that once softened the particular species of beauty that still thrives there. The trees also coloured the land, suffused the tarn in season with all the shades of spring, summer, autumn, the monochromes of winter; and they cheered it with spring and summer birdsong. The tarn also sees the vanished eagles, the much-longer-vanished wolves; knows for certain whether or not the relentlessly warming land and troublesomely milder winters will dissuade such as the whooper swans, drop-in geese, snow buntings, Scandinavian thrushes and goldeneyes from journeying so far south each autumn and winter. And when it sees (like you, like me) the red deer on Brock Crag, it also knows (because it sees what you and I do not see) that among the deer that drift down in the dusk and the full-blooded darkness to drink from the shore and the shallows, there are those that swim out to the islands to feed off the scraps of half-dead trees and ground-covering vegetation untroubled by sheep, there to nail down the hapless trees' coffins a little more securely.

The tarn sees with a clarity and an understanding far beyond the comprehension of all humankind what is at risk here.

A posse of goosanders cruised the tarn that day, supreme anglers (except that they only take what they need), casting for fish without need for rods, flies, bait, waders, jackets, nets, boats, just swimming the surface with their heads tilted forwards and their eyes underwater, primed to dive down.

A fish jumped on the far side of the tarn from the goosanders. The sunlight caught its tiny flight. I smiled. Thoreau again:

It may be that in the distance a fish describes an arc of three or four feet in the air, and there is one bright flash where it emerges, and another where it strikes the water; sometimes the whole silvery arc is revealed; or here and there, perhaps, is a thistledown floating on its surface, which the fishes dart at, and so dimple it again.

That Mr Thoreau – he was a bit of an Earth-eye himself. So one way or another, that's why Angle Tarn is special, why I remember it with affection from afar, why it rather got under my skin.

Nine

A Sense of Rightness Regained

THE STAGS ROARED from one side of Ullswater to the other. The answer was almost quick enough to have been an echo, but it was twice as long and ended in that stuttering cough which I always imagined was put there for emphasis, like exclamation marks or expletives. Open water is a wonderfully efficient conductor of sound. A master stag on Place Fell would resound all too clearly for the liking of his counterpart on the flanks of Glenridding, so regardless of the substantial body of water between them, he opened his throat and roared back. Logic would appear to play very little part in the intricacies of the red deer rut, but putting on a show is everything. Impress the hinds, humiliate the other stags. Roaring is designed to do both simultaneously, but the problem is always those stags that don't take no for an answer. The master stag stands his ground or at least he stands the ground where the hinds lead him. He is not really troubled by the roaring from across the water. But there are challengers on both sides of the lake and if they think their chances may be better served across the water, they can – and they do – swim across. So if an absence of logic might seem to afflict the master's behaviour, it's just that every time he fires off salvoes of raw noise into the mountain air, he is trying to hit more than one target.

It was an affecting moment for this deer-watcher at the start of the path between Patterdale and Hartsop. These were the first stags I had heard anywhere that autumn. Until that moment, I had only ever known the soundtrack of the rut as a Scottish chorale, for we suffer from a troublesome condition you could call "Monarch of the Glen Syndrome" – the Victorians have a hell of a lot to answer for. But I had not been in the Scottish mountains that particular autumn because of my commitments to the cause of this book, and I had simply not anticipated their presence in this landscape. I was caught unawares. But there is also this: in my accumulated decades watching and listening to the red deer's antheming of the autumn hills of home, there lurks the indelible memory of a more or less sleepless night camped on the mainland shore of the Sound of Sleat, with Skye across moonlit water. The stags on the slopes of Beinn Sgritheall, above the former home of Gavin Maxwell at Sandaig (his "Camusfearna", known to millions of readers of *Ring of Bright Water* around the world) had set up a call-and-response routine with others on Skye. It went on all night. And yes, the challengers can and they do swim across that narrow arm of the Atlantic at slack water.

Now on a bright Lakeland morning, the memory resurfaced, called back for one more curtain call by a substantial and sunlit stag that stood, Landseer-esque, on a small crag of Place Fell, and over my shoulder the shadowed and oak-shrouded unseen presence of his alter-ego across Ullswater. This cross-fertilisation in my mind, between this corner of Lakeland and various corners of Highland Scotland, was a constant companion during the pursuit of the particular wildness that has fed this book; a harking back and a harking forward, an invigorating blend of life-long familiarity and new discovery, so much that was new and different and enriching, so much that was common ground and reassuring. I decided right then that it was a good place to be, and I was captivated by the change of pace that Lakeland effected, the unfamiliar reference points, the slow opening up of the land to my explorations, the careful answers to my questions, the sudden surprise that united both worlds in a single gesture and stopped me dead, lost in a heady fusion of admiration and remembrance. What was John Muir's phrase at Wordsworth's graveside?

"A tear in my eye and a lump in my throat."

Such were the unpredictable consequences for me as the all-too-typical Scot lingering furth of his native heath. It was a wholly rewarding sensation. Just unexpected, unheralded.

★ ★ ★

Turning south at Side Farm, along the track to the village of Hartsop under the hills of Kirkstone Pass, had become another of my favourite Lakeland rituals. Big trees in big gardens closed in – monkey puzzles, Scots pines, oaks of every shape and size, the startling upstart scarlet of a Japanese maple – and I had stepped this way often enough by now to know some of these as individuals. Wrens seem to inhabit every other yard of stone wall here, which is a lot of yards. Given that it is a domestic architecture developed by humankind for their own exclusive needs, it is one more significant compliment to the hewers and stackers of stones that wrens find the results so much to their liking.

A primitive species of garden had been fashioned to the side of a trackside cottage by hacking level tiers into the raw hillside, each tier defined by a low stone-wall façade. Otherwise, untutored and untethered, hill grasses and other vegetation held sway, almost as before. I am no-one's idea of a gardener, but this hybrid between mountain and rudimentary horticulture was singularly appealing to me. But I passed it one sunlit late-January morning to find that its three tiers (effectively horizontal knee-high terraces) had been softened and startled and utterly transformed by equally horizontal ankle-high terraces of snowdrops, hundreds and hundreds of them crammed together above or below each terrace. The first thing I thought of was breaking waves, as though they might tumble down the terraces and come to rest in a constantly deepening pool of white the other side of the wall; constantly deepening, that is, until the snowdrops were done, withered and over and stashed away until the year's end when the green shoots reconvened and got their heads together again.

The second thing I thought of, then, was how much I like to encounter white in the landscape.

Apart from snow and swans (and you now know what Tunnicliffe thought of that!), it tends to be the fugitive presence of fleeting details: dipper bibs, the tails of bullfinches, sea eagles and hen harriers, waterfalls glimpsed among black crags, the retreating bouncing rumps of roe deer, the head of a summer snow bunting at 4,000 feet in the Cairngorms, midwinter ptarmigan, snowberries.

Snowdrops as densely packed as these are blatant brilliance.

You stare: they stare back.

En masse, they blaze.

But pick out a single plant that has strayed from the midst of the breaking wave – for they are an undisciplined bunch and forever slipping away from the mainstream, as lone wolves disavow the pack – and you might discern a certain cast of frailty there. A single snowdrop is nature's haiku, a self-contained miniature masterpiece without a shred of embellishment.

So the third thing I thought of was poetry. I know, I know, I am in Wordsworth country: I should worship at the shrine of "Daffodils". Yet where is Wordsworth's poem to snowdrops? Are they not as worthy – worthier? Well, at the risk of sounding heretical, the poet who springs to mind, the laureate of snowdrops, is Margiad Evans, unsung for much of her life and certainly ever since her death in 1958, except that I have been singing the praises of her deceptively titled *Autobiography* (Arthur Baker, 1943) for decades now. Deceptively titled, because it is not an autobiography in any conventional sense but rather an exquisite little volume of intensely personal nature writing from the England-Wales border country. Among its countless charms is an untitled poem, slipped into the narrative of the opening chapter, called "A Little Journal of Being Alone", and which is immediately preceded by this: "I love the alert freedom of being alone. Anything may come and you are ready to grasp it."

When night-time bars me in
and I am sitting sewing

my fancy takes the whim
to think of snowdrops growing,
they sprinkle grudging places
with slender drops of white,
and hang their orphan faces
in narrow hoods of light.
So frail I must recall
the shoulder of the cloud,
the scratching of the squall,
the wind, the frost, the flood.
Child kindness of the year
young promise of beguilement
more tender and more dear
than old fulfilment,
how strange it is to see
and hard to understand
your silver shine like charity
in winter's stubborn hand!

When I passed by that garden again a few weeks later, winter's stubborn hand had softened to spring's beckoning open palm, and while the snowdrops had shrunk to dull-green, ragged, ankle-high hedges that looked like nothing at all, farther along the lane where a verge of ankle-high grass was spring-thickening against the base of another stone wall fashioned from shallow-cut, horizontally-laid stones, and just where grass and wall met, there was a yellow-gold seam of – yes! – daffodils, gracing the morning. I fussed with a camera until I had a composition of horizontal thirds: dark Lakeland stone above, lush grass below, and the daffodils flirted right across the centre of the image, although each band trespassed and commingled with the others. For the duration, the daffodils had become landscape again, just as the snowdrops had done before them. After that, wherever I went along the track there were daffodils – in hosts, if you must. Somewhat bizarrely, I thought of the arrival of Arctic terns in Shetland, spring's true harbingers in northmost Britain: one day there are none at all, the next there are a few dozen, and the next again they are everywhere and the islands are transformed. On the way to Hartsop, there is a moment where the track curves round the bottom of a bank then climbs towards the shadowed corner of a field. The bank was a tumbledown of daffodils, a foreground crammed with yellows; and sunk deep in those background shadows stood a decrepit stone barn that deserves so much better than decrepitude, though it was arguably beautiful even in its neglect. I decided that, at their peak, daffodils reduce this corner of Lakeland to yellow and old stone. I also decided that I liked best that first impression, its scale miniature and spare, brief and pencil-thin, free from hosts. And since you asked, quite a few seasons after the event, my mind would revisit them, for they would still *flash upon that inward eye / Which is the bliss of solitude*. Strange how the phrase springs to your lips almost without trying. It is a very good poem, but then you knew that already.

But as so often happens in the hills of home, so it would be an autumn in this corner of Lakeland when the land and the day and the moment tilted into a new mood, one that lingers among those I hold closest of all these wanderings. The day dulled down from a clear early morning, then it tugged down a grey duvet of rain-filled cloud from mountainsides, clamped that onto a base level where it effectively became a ceiling just above the tree canopy, which in turn created an utterly redefined land ruled by the race of oak trees. As rain settled into a lightweight, airy presence, it also entered into a soft-voiced conspiracy with oak leaves, a million conversations. In response to the fineness of the rain, the oak leaves stirred into life and fluttered on the air a restless tricolor, an autumn-shaded banner of nature – fading green, deepening brown and searing yellow – which seemed to fuse everywhere I looked into an aura of dull gold. These are almost the perfect conditions in which to consider the passage of autumn through a grove of old oaks, for they remove all the distractions of sunlight and wide visibility, and the gloss of light rain enlivens the shades of every leaf. My old artist friend, George Garson, who still keeps creeping into my thoughts and my books a decade after his death, told me to go and look at stained glass windows only on days when the light had this kind of smoored softness, and not to bother on a sunny day. It is the sunless days that permit the glass to be its own sunlight. He knew what he was talking about: he had his own department at Glasgow School of Art and he specialised in murals and stained glass.

He had his gods, but they were all painters, and one of them was Paul Nash. Thanks to George I became familiar with Nash's landscapes, especially his trees. So, given that George was already in my thoughts, it was no surprise to me that Nash came quietly to mind and stood beside him. The oaks were at their thickest where they gathered on low knolls above Goldrill Beck, the river that trembles quietly all through the floor of the valley from Brothers Water to Ullswater. On one of those knolls in particular, the trees seemed so stylised and apparently thoughtfully composed as a group that it looked as if Paul Nash had put them there so that he could paint them. He sometimes referred to his hilltop trees as "clumps", which almost seemed unkind, considering the elegance with which he painted his trees, and the insinuations of a kind of eeriness. I thought of christening this particularly conspicuous knoll Nash's Clump, then thought better of the idea and came up with Knash's Knot, which I like much better, and in my personal geography of Lakeland, Knash's Knot it remains.

There was a wistfulness about the atmosphere among the oaks that day, the lightness of the rain amounting to no more than a hoarse whisper; something felt but unseen, and comforting rather than discomfiting, as if perhaps nature herself had decided to go for a walk in the woods and washed up here. This notion of something other in landscape is hardly a new one. Gerard Manley Hopkins called it the "inscape", a landscape of the mind that lurks within the physical landscape. Nash knew it, too, and constantly tried to find a way of incorporating it into the way he painted. A reviewer of a Tate exhibition in 2016 to commemorate the 60th anniversary of his death wrote that his "transformations of reality were the product of a visionary sensibility that harked back to William Blake and Samuel Palmer; he searched for inner meanings in the landscape, what he called the 'things behind'". But Nash was a modernist, too, and the European drift towards abstraction and surrealism intrigued him. There is a tangible sense of melancholy in many of his landscapes, but then he was a war artist in both world wars, and surely that would layer the way he painted forever. Given that I had subconsciously started to create a mental collage of guiding lights and inspirations that have illuminated my writing life, Gavin Maxwell drifted into mind then, a passage from the autobiography of his child-hood, *The House of Elrig* (Longmans, 1965), in which he writes of his mother:

> *In all her appreciation of beauty there was that which I either inherited or acquired from her, an inherent approach of mel-ancholy or nostalgia, so that splendour could not be splendid were it not desolate too.*

I have wondered since how long I spent on Knash's Knot that day. It could have been an hour, it could have been three. The day was briefly beyond time. Landscape is the basis of more or less everything I write, my rock, my foun-dation stone, upon which all else is built. Wherever I go to work, the land beneath my feet is a constant awareness. The raw stuff of the planet seeps into the writing process. On that unsung eminence, unnamed until I christened it (but don't expect Knash's Knot to appear on O.S. maps any time soon), I happened on it at a fugitive moment in its story. Aided by the passage of Goldrill Beck below, the sense of the tug of the valley's final glacial struggles reached up through the oak roots where I sat. When a glacier departs finally from such a valley, acknowledging the hopelessness of trying to unseat the immovable object in its path and, in the same moment, further acknowledging that its force is no longer irresistible, does it leave something of itself behind? For sure, its signature is all over the rocks, but have those same rocks trapped something of its energy – energy that was, after all, sufficient to reorganise the nature of the land and command it to shift, mountains to bow down and yield? And is that energy what an artist taps into when he comes in his own time, questing for "inscapes", for "things behind"? What went through George Garson's mind when, on a holiday on the island of Luing in the Firth of Lorne, he felt for the first time the slate of that Argyll shore in his hands and considered its possibilities as a material for his mosaics, and a material that, in his art at least, could stand in for the bedrock of Orkney, where all his roots lay?

Another of my friends, writer and mountaineer David Craig (an Aberdonian, who found a rewarding home from home just a few miles down the road from Knash's Knot at Burton-in-Kendal whence he travelled to work as professor of creative writing at Lancaster University), introduced his matchless mountaineering book, *Native Stones* (Secker and Warburg, 1987), with a quotation from an exhibition in Leeds City Art Gallery in 1985, entitled "Henry Moore: Sculpture in the Making":

As a young man Moore preferred the native stones, believing that as an Englishman he should understand them. His choice of brown Hornton stone from Edgehill in Oxfordshire for the Leeds Reclining Figure, a material with fossil remains, pronounced veins of iron ore and colours varying from light brown to greenish blue, enabled him to express his idea of

figure sculpture as landscape. The extremities are treated like
sunlit hills with a valley in shadow between them and veins
like contours on a map.

In the same book, in an opening essay on the lure of
climbing rock that I must have read fifty times, David wrote:

It all happens at a pace that can be remembered: as delib-
erately as a work of art shaping under your pen or brush or
mallet; as lengthily as a night when one dream dissolves into
the next and none of them are forgotten; as concentratedly as
a spell of watching to see an animal. The gradual, trudging
hours peak into an instant revelation – there it is (the roe
deer, the eagle) – the lovely image manifests itself – your
mind snaps it for good – then nature lapses back into its
immense quietude.

And this:

But when I sit on a six-inch ledge with my feet dangling
above a two hundred-foot drop, the hart's-tongue fern and
dwarf hawthorn a few inches from my eye, the air smelling
of moss, wood-pigeons clattering out of the tree-tops down
below, then at least for a time I have grafted myself back into
nature, and the sense of rightness achieved, or regained, is
unmistakable.

There it is: the sense of rightness achieved, or regained.
Is that what unites all these questing artists in whose shad-
owy footsteps I have wandered? For it was never enough

for me just to go into wild country, reach the mountaintop, pronounce it climbed, then descend back into that other life. When, in 1988, I resigned from my job as a newspaper journalist and sailed to St Kilda to write my first book, I had the absurd notion that the work would become the life, the life would become the work, and nature – the land itself – would keep me afloat. And that way I would have the time to indulge my inclinations, and these were to achieve my own sense of rightness, to live nature, become the landscape I moved through, and regain that sense of rightness each time I went back. And then write down what that felt like.

It stopped raining.

In the instant the whisperers were gone, the sound of the beck rushed into the space where they had been, a flypast of waxwings paused to cluster in the canopy. For the first time in who-knows-how-long there was a focal point rather than an atmosphere. With the arrival of the birds and the end of the rain something was lost from all that had gone before. But my mind still went rummaging among the shades and visitations of figures who, one way or another, had turned my head and made me think while I admired them for the path they had chosen, and having chosen, set out to find a different angle of vision, their own sense of rightness. All these had arrived as if their gathering was pre-ordained, so that while I gleaned raw material for a new idea of wildness in a landscape I was only slowly getting to know, they were there to remind me of their influence, their teachings, and they had lent their voices to the whispering of the rain and the leaves, so that the trees themselves heard and responded. And I was there to bear witness, to listen.

More or less as I began to write this chapter, news reached me of the death of the American writer Barry Lopez. He was one of the giants of my trade. There is a passage in his book, *Arctic Dreams* (Scribners, 1986), I have almost learned by heart, and now that the mood of the day was changing and I was looking more thoughtfully at that piece of land and why I had responded to it so intensely, it was Lopez that I reached for:

> *Whatever evaluation we finally make of a stretch of land, no matter how profound or accurate, we will find it inadequate. The land retains an identity of its own, still deeper and more subtle than we can know. Our obligation toward it then becomes simple: to approach with an uncalculating mind, with an attitude of regard. To try to sense the range and variety of its expression — its weather and colour and animals. To intend from the beginning to preserve some of the mystery within it as a kind of wisdom to be experienced, not questioned. And to be alert for its openings, for that moment when something sacred reveals itself within the mundane, and you know that the land knows you are there.*

* * *

A mile along the track, where the oaks relented and the hillside was comparatively open, there was a solitary wayside birch. As birch trees go (and I stand among the world's admirers of silver birches, think them among the most elegant and stylish of native trees and only a willow weeps to equally emotion-toying effect), it was as unremarkable as any I have ever seen: short and squat and unweeping and unwillowy. A casual passer-by caring more for looks than the niceties of silviculture might have said it looked tired. Except…except that its upper reaches looked agitated, in a fidgety way. That was why I gave it a second glance – it fidgeted. It also flashed sporadically and tinily and all over its upper reaches, pinpoints of yellow, as if it had been invaded by hundreds of glowworms. At fifty yards away it created the impression of having downcast its standard-issue crock of autumn gold only to have re-attired itself in a tartan plaid of green, grey, white, black and – especially – those tiny shards of yellow that darted like forked lightning. On such a flat, monochrome, tranquil, windless day, it contrived to rock and mutter and squeak as if a truculent breeze was busy there, but only there in all that landscape.

The whole intriguing illusion was the work of something like 200 siskins. Their restless, fluttering bustle was all the more watchable because so much of it was conducted upside-down. It takes your eyes a while – even through the lenses of good binoculars – to decipher the meaning of the yellow lightning. It is not just that the yellow in the siskin's plumage is so vivid, it is also set off by black. If you home in on a single bird – say, a male with its back to you and its head turned to one side (it's watching you watching it) – what leaps into focus is a Fabergé bird. There is a J-shaped swirl of yellow on the side of its head, reaching back from the black eye and beneath the black crown, curving down to where its neck would be if it had a neck worth the name. Two more yellow curves, one on each of its folded wings, each lined above and below with curves of black. When the wings open in flight, the two curves extend and meet in an elegant, flattened W-shape. Below that, and to the sides of its upper edges, there is a wingtip-to-wingtip fan of tiny vertical black and yellow bands. A further diamond of yellow reveals itself on the bird's back when the wings open, and again it's bounded with black, and the black tail with its distinctive fork is underpinned with yet more yellow. Multiply all of the above by 200, the result compounded by the fact that every one of them is a constant shifting of tiny movements, often involving wings opening and closing, heads turning, tails flirting…the whole thing can entertain a susceptible mortal for as long as the birds feel inclined to plunder the rapidly diminishing store of catkins.

And then they flew.

Was there a signal?

Was there an instruction about direction?

There was no apparent cause for alarm, no peregrine on the skyline, no knee-high sparrowhawk carving a furrow through the airspace above the path. I hadn't moved in fifteen minutes. But they flew on the instant, all of them at once, as densely packed as snow crystals in a snowball. And they all flew north, so almost straight above me. The surprise was a muted roar. If you see a single siskin in flight, there is very little sound. But 200 pairs of wings seem somehow to amount to an infinitely greater outcome than the sum of the parts. It was electrifying, it was startling. The flight was short, and described a perfect anti-clockwise oval, straight back to the same birch where it had started. Two hundred landings produced not a single false move, not a single dispute for any particular two-inch piece of twig.

Within seconds, all movement was reduced to the flock's characteristic perched fidget. They fed in silence.

How different from that flock of fifty, 1,800 feet up on the ridge of Ard Crags above Keskadale. Every trait of their behaviour was transformed. On Ard Crags, the flock was loose and freewheeling and scattered to feed on hill grasses over a hundred yards. Their constant short flights from one patch of grass to another were full of contact calls. They were relaxed, almost certainly a migrating flock on the move. Here, more than a thousand feet lower, the flock was tight-packed and flew as a unit. Its brief flight out from the tree, a 200-yard round trip back into the tree again, was almost like watching a single creature with a voice that roared in the air, but softly. Over the next fifteen or twenty minutes, they flew twice more, action replays of the first flight with the same result. Again, there was no obvious reason for the flights, no obvious source of disturbance. I decided to move on, which would mean walking past the tree. I passed five or six yards away. Not a single bird flinched. After a hundred yards I stopped to look back. All was as before. The tree fidgeted. Its bird-horde seemed determined to strip it of every last morsel of siskin food. It was the discipline of the thing that took me aback then: the reasoning power involved that discovered the food source of the solitary tree and devised an instant system by which the entire flock could profit. You might stumble on the Ard Crags flock, with that wide-open expanse of hill grasses and their seeds at its disposal, and conclude that *that* was how a migrating siskin flock sustained itself, and without thinking about it too deeply, treat that single encounter as definitive. But the more you immerse yourself in pursuit of wildness and the more thoughtful the immersion, whether in Lakeland or anywhere else on Earth, the more you learn that (as we like to say ourselves, distantly echoing our own hunting past) there is more than one way to skin a rabbit. An increasing and lamentable tendency to take our learning from field guides rather than from out in the field saddles us with the idea that every member of a single species behaves the same way. And yet, in the total absence of field guides, someone like Burns knew better than that more than two centuries ago, or for that matter, someone like Wordsworth:

> *Come forth into the light of things,*
> *Let Nature be your teacher.*
> *She has a world of ready wealth,*
> *Our minds and hearts to bless –*
> *Spontaneous wisdom breathed by health,*
> *Truth breathed by chearfulness...*
> *Come forth, and bring with you a heart*
> *That watches and receives.*

Siskins, more than most creatures, have prospered from Britain's modern forestry industry. Its relatively small bill is adept at prising seeds from trees like Sitka spruce and larch, the industry's two great staples. That factor, and that alone, is responsible for the improvement in the siskin's UK fortunes in the last 100 years, and especially in the last fifty. If Wordsworth had seen that flock in the birch tree, and known that such a prosperous flock and its spectacle was the product of plantation forestry, might he have revised his sentiments about the arrival of larch in the Lake District, of which, you may remember, he wrote: "To those who plant for profit, and they are thrusting every other tree out of the way, to make way for their favourite, the larch, I would first utter a regret that they should have selected these lovely vales for their vegetable manufactory." I am no fan of industrial-scale monoculture, but every now and again, there is an object lesson to be learned about nature's capacity to insinuate wildness into the unlikeliest of circumstances. You discover them and you learn them when you come forth into the light of things and let nature be your teacher.

★ ★ ★

All the way to the waterfall where Angle Tarn Beck effects a final mountainside gesture before diving down under the track and slithering away across flattening fields to swell the ranks of Goldrill Beck's northward march towards Ullswater, the day began to lift and enliven. Something like sunlight loosened the burden of clouds on the big tops clustered around that rift in the hills reaching from Ullswater to Kirkstone Pass. Cofa Pike above Deepdale emerged razor-edged and snow-capped, and over half an hour so did the entire arch from whiter-still Helvellyn to Fairfield, Hart Crag to Stony Cove Pike. Snow had touched them all. And all the while I could still hear in my head the throaty tumult of siskin wings that had become the signature of the day.

I have always liked to keep the company of waterfalls. There is first the voice in which it announces its presence from a distance, often unseen; that voice that deepens and darkens in spate, and lightens and loses its bass tones when prolonged summer sun or winter ice make their presence felt. But pass some time on its banks, listen hard, and hear the disparate voices of everything from its greatest leap to its softest, slowest lisp through an inches-deep crack, a pool whispering out of the corner of its mouth; and every voice in that ragged-edged symphony has its pitch, its dizzy semi-quavers, its long legatos and demented pizzicatos, its horns and clarinets, piccolos and bassoons, its cellos, snare drums and kettle drums. Who stops to listen to the acoustic layers of a mountain waterfall? Who lends an ear to nature's language? Should it not be a duty of all who come here in pursuit of whatever it is that the fells, becks, tarns, lakes, woods give them, to then listen to what the land has to say, to what nature needs from you. You are, after all, an animal too, you are nature yourself, so does it not follow that if you would have nature serve your cause, then you should be prepared to serve nature's in return?

It is my experience that making a space in a mountain day to look around, linger, listen, pay attention to where you are, its detail as well as its grand gestures; to think about whether the land where you are looks well or weary, in good heart or worn to the bone…that spending some time in quiet contemplation of nature's world is more revealing than any mountaintop panorama. More revealing, that is, of nature's mindset. But why bother? Why not turn up, seek, find, climb your mountain and go home again, pleased with yourself that you came and saw and conquered, grateful perhaps that your town-or-city-beleaguered spirits were lightened, however briefly, sure in the knowledge that when you come back the fells will still be there when you need them? Is that not enough? I think that no, it is not enough to come and go and be glad. I think it has become necessary to understand. A tract of country as overrun by people as Lakeland has become and as beleaguered by sheep, as wounded by the relentless and ever-increasing demands of our species, begins to lose its capacity to heal. Tourism is essentially a selfish and greedy industry that measures success in terms of visitor numbers and revenues. Wherever and however it advances, nature retreats before it, wildness falters, and more often than not it withers and dies.

So I think it is worthwhile to stop and listen, worthwhile to question the role of our species in what we see and what we hear when nature's voice is troubled, restless, unsettled, distraught.

No time is wasted in nature's company when we spend it passively, and watch nature at work.

★ ★ ★

As sunlight fired up the land and the late autumn-in-to-winter colours, letting shadows and definition in among the isolated stands and whole woodlands of oak, a new shadow threw a dark band across the nearest field to the waterfall. It was the shadow of a drystone wall. The wall had obviously been there the whole time, but in the flat light before the sun emerged, it had simply made no impact on the landscape. The sunlight laid down the shadow in two distinct tones. One, the solid black band, was the unlit side of the wall itself. The other was the paler shadow the wall cast on the ground. But the sun also lit the crest of the wall. So where the wall had been a band of dull grey, attracting neither attention nor admiring glance, within a single transforming moment it attracted both. It also became a component part of a suddenly revealed Lakeland jewel, in which landscape and built stone fused in common cause and made nothing less than art itself.

The gently sloping land below that part of the track to Hartsop was given over to that species of farmland kindly referred to as "marginal", which more or less means that it will feed sheep but it's not much use for anything else. Old stone walls carved the slope into three fields. Immediately below the track, the slope had been divided into two small fields. The lower slope was a much larger field, which was as wide as the combined width of the two upper fields. To follow the line of the wall that had first caught my eye is to be led to the centrepiece of a landscape composition as arresting and aesthetically satisfying as anything in that whole brightening panorama that reached across the valley and beyond to the very heights of Helvellyn. At its far end, the wall met the side of a stone barn at right angles. The wall dividing the two small fields also met the barn at right angles, but at the rear gable end. So one beautifully proportioned barn set so comfortably into the hillside that it looked as if it might have grown organically there, served the needs of three fields.

But nature had moved in when no one was looking, doubtless attracted by the sheltered aspect of the uphill-facing corner where the sunlit-and-shadow wall met the barn. Perhaps a hundred years ago now, two Scots pines had seeded there, and demonstrably they have prospered. The crown of their two-fold canopy towered about sixty feet above the ridge of the barn's roof, but their trunks were less than six feet apart. The foliage of their lower branches threw a mottled patchwork of sunlight and shadow all across the stonework and slate of the near side of the barn. A light breeze, newly sprung, animated the whole building, so that it was briefly uncanny. If neither the barn nor the field walls had ever been built and the pines had never sought sanctuary there, you would still pronounce that view as fair. But it would be a hard-hearted member of the species of humankind – even the most uncompromising of nature writers – who could deny that in that singular corner of Lakeland, humankind and nature had conspired to ennoble the lie of the land.

The sentiment was endorsed and underlined by a stoat. My view of the near end of the sunlight-and-shadow wall was screened by a bank of bushes. The stoat emerged from beyond them, running along the top of the wall. To my certain knowledge, there are three reasons why a stoat likes to run along the top of a drystone wall. One is that there may be mice inside the wall. Another is that there may be small birds inside the wall – wrens, for example. The third is... just for the hell of it. I have seen a brood of newly fledged wrens explode from the innards of such a wall as this with a stoat clattering along their roof, and I have witnessed a stoat chase a field mouse in and out of such a wall, the denouement infuriatingly concealed when it was resolved one way or the other on the blind side of the wall. But then there was this Lakeland wall, all 100 yards of it (my hasty guess), and the stoat was running in the direction of the barn.

I locked the glasses on it as it ran, and every other stride was a leap across a chasm between stones, none of them very wide as chasms go, but almost all of them capable of accommodating a squirming stoat, and therefore, if it missed its footing just once, of breaking one or more of its legs. But nothing flew or scampered from the wall and the stoat just ran and ran and ran and did not hesitate once and did not miss its footing once, although sometimes its body was at full stretch and sometimes it was arched so tightly that it looked painful, yet it still ran. It was almost at the barn when it started to curve to the left, and only then did I realise that the wall did not meet the barn at right angles at all, but rather curved away from its dead straight course at the very end...*to accommodate the two pines.* And now I am left wondering what came first – the wall or the trees. My best guess is this. The wall came first. It did meet the barn at right angles, then the trees arrived, and as they grew they threatened the stability of the wall, and rather than fell the trees (which would be the gut reaction of some landowners I can think of), the end of the wall was taken down and rebuilt, in deference to the grace of the Scots pines.

And what happened to the stoat? I don't know. I was lost in admiration and wonder for the gesture of the builders of walls that work so thoughtfully with nature they become landscape themselves.

★ ★ ★

The following day, I walked the other way, from Hartsop to Knash's Knot, where the day ground to a halt in a golden, sunlit dream. Lunch was the best kind of lunch, with my back to a venerable oak. It was on the top of the Knot, with a view that drifted down through a screen of oak limbs, branches, twigs and twiglets and the late-autumn sorcery of oak leaves, to the slippery course of Goldrill Beck as it navigated the base of the Knot. A patch of sunlight blazed off the water. Over an hour, that blaze advanced round a bend in the river and through a patch of white water, which turned liquid gold as the sun passed through. The deep lime-green glow of moss-thickened oak trunks and limbs added nature's most vivid shade of green to the palette of woodland and water. The soundtrack of the hour was of red deer stags roaring on the hillside behind me and, again, these were echoed from the far side of the valley. I sat with a notebook and a fountain pen, scribbling the notes that became the basis for these pages, and reminded myself that there are days when I think perhaps I have the best job in the world, and this was one of them.

A flock of long-tailed tits invaded the oaks and because I was sitting still when they arrived and remained still, they treated me as a scrap of the woodland, which is to say they ignored me altogether. Over about ten minutes they flickered in ones, twos and small groups into the immediate foreground of the oak screen, all of them backlit by the sun from above and below where it flared off the water. Eventually, there were between fifty and sixty, and the wood glistened with their constant high-pitched, three-and-four-syllable calls, so constant it was like an exquisite silver rain.

As a counterpoint to the brute strength of stag-bellow, there can be very little else in the natural vocabulary of all Lakeland that is quite so intimate, but it was the product of so many opened throats, and because these were constantly overlapping. They amounted to a freewheeling campanology of the flimsiest bells you ever heard. I wondered if the gutturals of the stags registered with them at all, if they understood what they signified, or if the deer were so beyond their everyday preoccupations that they paid them no more heed than they did to my shape at the foot of one more oak. Strange to think that these charmers of the woodland edge were devouring beetles, spiders, flies and the eggs of moths and butterflies, even as they charmed. But everything has to eat, and the fact that long-tails have become bird table regulars in the gardens of the land in the last few decades should not obscure the fact that this is where they are at home, quite literally, for many flocks work their own feeding territories through the autumn and winter. For them, your bird feeder comes in handy when the oak tree larders are midwinter-bare.

There was a fence inside the oak wood. It crossed the dome of Knash's Knot from east to west. What looked very much like a badger track followed a parallel course nearby. With lunch hour over (it overran, as usual), the track offered a natural way back down the Knot. Instead, I found my way barred by a red squirrel. This takes a bit of believing. I am six feet tall in my walking boots. The squirrel was standing on the ground and less than a foot tall. It was angry. It did not approve of me being there at all. There was earth on its nose and feet. Autumn is when it harvests acorns and lays them in for the winter in caches in the ground. This one had just been caught in the act. A surprisingly loud stream of sound voiced extreme disapproval as self-evidently as if it had deployed 21st-century Anglo-Saxon. The impasse lasted perhaps two minutes. It ended when the squirrel decided on discretion rather than valour. It ran at the nearest oak, leapt for the trunk, hit it several feet above the ground and began running vertically in the same instant. It turned onto the first limb and ran halfway, where it stopped and screeched again. The trouble was that the limb led nowhere. That galvanised one of the most extraordinary cameos of virtuosic agility I have ever seen in all nature.

The squirrel doubled back to the trunk and sprinted vertically up to the fork, where it took the left-hand limb. This climbed almost as steeply as the trunk. High in the canopy, it selected what was surely the longest branch on the tree and, still running without pause, it followed the branch to its outermost reaches. Just before the integrity of the branch disintegrated into a maze of twigs, the squirrel took off. I hesitate to guess how far it flew through the air, but it made a perfect landing on a branch of the next tree, and hit it running. Now that it was high, it stayed high. Its flight from whatever danger it perceived in my intrusion on its acorn-caching ritual became a flat-out, high-level, high-octane sprint that seemed to be conducted as much in the air as on a tree. It fled through one canopy after another and I was able to follow it in binoculars for fully a hundred yards. It was still going when there was simply too much standing timber in the way for me to track it. I was aware that I was smiling, that I felt like laughing for the sheer joy of the watching and, simultaneously, like apologising for inducing such a response. If I were Robert Burns I would be writing something called "To A Red Squirrel", for I had just inflicted one more breach in nature's social union, for all that I had been as unwitting as Burns when his plough trashed the mouse's winter nest.

All the way back to Hartsop, I kept replaying the squirrel's part in the day, from the moment it stood on its hind legs with dirt on its nose and front paws and swore at me for several seconds, until I lost sight of its flouncing tail half a woodland away. I interrupted the reverie twice: once when I passed the siskin tree (not a bird in sight but the symphony of small wings seemed to have left an eerie echo on the air), and again when I passed the waterfall and turned to look at the wall, the barn, the pines, wondered about the stoat.

And then I wondered if these might just be nature's favourite miles in all England.

Ten

Ash to Ashes

BROTHERS WATER LAPPED UP the light of sunshine after rain, infused with smoky leftovers of clouds that still clung to summit, ridge and buttress, bright white rags just robust enough to scatter shadows in confetti profusion. So instead of the dazzle of unfettered sunlight on the smallest lake in Lakeland, there was a quiet sheen on the surface that suggested mother-of-pearl. Accidents of geography, geology and glaciology have conferred on Brothers Water a visual impact out of all proportion to its size. If it lay anywhere else other than on the valley floor, it would have been a tarn. In Scotland, it would be a lochan rather than a loch. From high on the south shoulder of Place Fell, looking south towards Kirkstone Pass, the handsome mountains that made a skittish road over the pass necessary in the first place were having their thunder stolen again. And while there was no denying their captivating aspect, in one sense they were the cause of their own downfall, for north-facing aspects extended long, broad, wooded ridges and buttresses towards the valley floor, sheltering arms surely designed to safeguard their offspring (Brothers Water is nature's child of all their valleys), and your eye is inclined to keep slipping again and again from the high tops to the scene-stealer. Brothers Water's misshapen diamond is a pearl among sumptuous oysters, a still centre amid the tumult of that arc of mountains.

Close up, there is a glacial quality to Brothers Water, hardly surprising as its feeding waters flow from Hart Crag, Scandale Fell, Kirkstone Pass and Stony Cove Pike, short and fast mountain waters all. They only pause for breath when they finally coalesce and reach the flat ground immediately to the south of the lake, where human hands and human mindset have straightened the single watercourse that finally flows into Brothers Water, just as they have tampered with the course of Goldrill Beck, which flows out of it. It's all slightly disappointing, anti-climactic, for the whole head of the valley must once have been a wonderful wooded wetland, and wouldn't it be refreshing to hear that the national park authority, mindful of its World Heritage status, has taken the bold and visionary decision to restore such a wetland? But I suspect that hell will freeze over before that happens, and given the way things are going with our ever-warming climate, hell freezing over is simply out of reach until nature contrives the next ice age. Notwithstanding all that, apart from the reed bed at its south edge and a patch of aquatic vegetation at its outflow (the birth throes of Goldrill Beck), Brothers Water is cold and clear and bare. There was a furtive glimpse of a mute swan in the reed bed, which I like to think was one of the pair I met on Angle Tarn. It takes a great deal to persuade a mute swan pair to abandon an established nest site, but I wonder if global warming might induce such a drastic change some future spring or other, and perhaps they will bring the offspring down to Brothers Water for the winter?

Low Wood cloaks a long curving wedge of the lowest slopes of all that land between Deepdale and Dovedale. I fell hard for Dovedale at first sight. Seven skinny tributaries feed a beck that has its source at around 800 metres and just below the summit of Hart Crag. One more lazy lunch with my back to an ancient oak right on the bank was simply a delectable hour of drinking in the companionship of a profound sense of place, a connection that was both instant and intimate and consequently rare. On the easy slopes just above the beck are two hawthorns destined to live long in the mind of anyone who craves the individuality of trees. One was hoisted on a low and stubby trunk, with a canopy in the shape of a shallow dome that was almost perfectly circular and twice as wide as the tree was high. The shapeliness was what caught the eye first, but what held it was the relationship it achieved with a recumbent slab of rock like a collapsed standing stone or an uncarved grave of one of those timeless heroes of legend that date back to when the world was young. That relationship was such that it looked as if the tree had taken on itself the role of protector, so that the slab was perpetually in its shade. Tree and rock contrived a simplistic beauty, against a backdrop of the climbing walls and woods and waterfalls of Dovedale. I would love to see that tree in blossom. The second hawthorn was as berserk as the first was beautiful, for it appeared to be hell-bent on tying itself in knots. The trunk was substantial and straightforward and obviously of great age, as hawthorns go. The problem began at the fork. The left fork climbed steeply away from the trunk but then unaccountably bent at right angles and was so twisted as to head into the centre of the tree instead of outwards to spread a canopy. But still more bizarrely, the right-hand fork did exactly the same thing, but in the opposite direction. The result was that in time, the branches these forks produced have overlapped, and in some cases fused. The right-hand fork, having made its right angle bend, then forked again, and into that second fork rose the realigned left fork. You can see where this is going. But one way or another, there never was such a tree.

Once the course of Dovedale Beck starts to climb and open out, the view sprawls across Low Wood. It had been a benevolent, storm-free autumn thus far and much of the oak wood foliage was still green and growing. But something was not right. All over the wood, tall trees reaching above the oak canopy were bare of leaves and whitened. The impact in such a place of wild beauty was a troubling one. What I was seeing was the frightening spoor of ash dieback.

This catastrophe-in-the-making has a salutary story. It is a wind-borne disease caused by a fungus. It originated in China, where it has caused comparatively little damage. (What does that remind you of?) It found its way to mainland Europe thirty years ago, and Britain was rather slow on the uptake. (What does that remind you of?) For reasons known to smarter people than me, Britain went on importing thousands of ash plants from infected areas of Europe until 2012, when the trade was banned – twenty-two years too late. Our native ash did not evolve with the fungus so has no natural defence against it. Year-on-year infections will simply kill it. The fungus restricts the movement of water through the tree, which is essential for the growth of timber and foliage. Leaf loss and bark lesions follow then the tree starts to crack.

How important is this in the greater scheme of things? Well, the ash is Britain's third most common native tree. Dappled ground cover, a characteristic of ash woods, fosters ground plants essential to teeming populations of invertebrates, and therefore to birds and mammals that feed on them. The two places that really hurt when the natural food chain is damaged are the very top and the very bottom. One human consideration: the importance of ash to the manufacture of furniture, tools, instruments. The clean-up operation will include the need for felling dangerous roadside and railway line woods, woods in urban areas. Then, given the importance of the tree to our ecosystem, there is the matter of replanting. If you must put a figure on such a monster, you're in luck, as the magazine *Current Biology* has already done it: as near as makes no difference, the bill is £15 billion. But that afternoon in Low Wood in Dovedale, it was simply the moment when a day of varied natural delights was involved in a head-on collision with a Chinese tree-eating monster that bruises the heart and puts a foul taste in the mouth. It felt as if the day was getting away from me, when suddenly there was an odd meeting of three buzzards above the wood.

Buzzards are familiar enough in Lakeland and such a wood is ideal habitat. It was the sound of raised buzzard voices that lifted my head, and when I saw two buzzards in vertical pursuit of a third, I lifted my binoculars. My first thought was that October is an odd time of year for a dispute over territory. Buzzards, like golden eagles, tend to relax territorial boundaries once the young are flying, and lazy, thermalling gatherings of anything up to a dozen birds are a feature of autumn and early-winter skies. This did not look at all like that. Second thought: the pursuers were almost certainly an established pair, the female noticeably bigger than the male as they dived almost wingtip to wingtip. Again judging by size, the pursued bird was a second male, but something about it didn't quite fit. Sunlight suggested a pale head, but its flight was in and out of the canopy and it was some minutes before I had a clear view. Buzzard plumage is notoriously variable and I was wary of jumping to conclusions in such circumstances, especially the one that was already desperate to jump from the back of my mind to the front. Then the chase burst out of the canopy, climbing steeply with the pair a couple of yards behind the intruder and apparently more interested in seeing it off the premises than launching an attack. As the pursued bird climbed, sunlight showed me clearly what I had hoped I might see: a white tail with a black tip. It was a rough-legged buzzard, only the second I had ever seen. The few we see in Britain are Scandinavians, mostly Norwegian, mostly on the east coast, mostly they arrive in October. Their presence is sporadic and usually suggests a food shortage on their home range. Numbers are small in any one British winter – single figures, sometimes tens, with very occasionally an influx of over a hundred. Whatever, it is a rare beast in Lakeland, and I doubt if I would have given it a second glance without the significant protest of the natives.

So my third thought is that the native pair, although they were not motivated by territorial factors and would normally be well enough disposed towards others of their own tribe, recognised the rough-legged buzzard as an alien presence and resolved to send it on its way, which suggests a sophisticated familiarity with the contents of what I still tend to think of as *The Observer's Book of Birds*, for all that a wheen of bird books have passed through my hands since I had one of those. It was the first of all my bird books as a child of seven or eight, and everything else has simply been a sophistication of its essential simplicity. Those essentials are all that a pair of Lakeland buzzards would require, that and the greater essential of living life as Lakeland buzzards. I take a decidedly non-twitching attitude to birds, for my preoccupation is with all nature, but like anyone else for whom nature is a way of life, there is an undeniable thrill when you cross the path of a rarity, whether bird or beast, fish or flower, supermoon or aurora borealis. The fact that the rough-legged buzzard and I were both wanderers from more northerly climes layered the moment with a dash of fellow feeling.

Eleven

Divining in Reverse

A LINE in the grim beauty of the prologue in Sarah Hall's novel, *Haweswater* (Faber, 2002), caught my eye and held it, so that having admired it, I went back to see how she had slipped it into its sentence with such precision. The line is this:

> *…he found himself divining in reverse, looking for old land…*

"He" is Samuel Lightburn, farmer at Mardale Green. He is bidding farewell to his village, even as it drowns. It is 1937. They have built the dam so that Manchester might slake its thirst for water (a thirst that would soon prove insatiable), and they have begun to flood his valley, his farm, his house, his home. He is coaxing his horse and cart through the rising waters, dragging away a last meagre cargo of hay. He can see "three ruptured buildings". Then you read this:

> *In a matter of days or weeks they would be submerged, but for now they rose from the water-like pieces of grey bone and he found himself divining in reverse, looking for old land.*

The line had come back to me while I pored over old photographs of the village of Mardale Green before the dam was built – the undrowned village – and tried to reconcile what the photographs enshrined with what the

21st-century valley had become, which is a cul-de-sac for tourists. The village still resurrects occasionally, or at least it contrives a ghastly apparition of itself whenever drought conditions prevail, although droughts in Lakeland are thinner on the ground than blue moons in its sky, and mostly the remains of the old stone walls are sunk deep beneath the blue-grey meniscus of a reservoir called Haweswater.

If I confess to unease at the task I had set myself here, it is because I am no Samuel Lightburn. This is not my native heath. I don't "belong" to this land, as we would say in that land to which I do belong. It almost feels like tampering with someone else's geology. And yet there was something about Mardale Head that took hold of me and, having taken hold, held on.

What?

Not the obvious hit-you-between-the-eyes mountain scrum of Harter Fell, High Street, Kidsty Pike and their cohorts, rubbing hunched, muscular shoulders with each other and cramping the airspace for headroom. Not that. It is an impressive enough refuge for Haweswater's headwaters, but there are more impressive mountain gatherings in Lakeland than that one. And not the human history either: the overwhelming of a local tribe and their local landscape and the rituals and the traditions and the beauties of both before Manchester's drouth overcame the rights of a landscape and a community just to be, to exist, to flourish. But whenever were considerations like that a factor in the vexed history of the Lake District National Park, which continues to vex to this day?

What then?

Again and again as I rummaged among those black and white photographs, they showed a conspicuous, shapely little hill that rose from the midst of the village. A stone wall ran right across its summit, bisecting its simple conical shape. To one side of the wall the slope was covered with what looked like a conifer plantation. The other side was quite bare. I thought that it must have been framed in every other window in Mardale Green, thought about how it must have carved a place for itself into the mind of every Mardale native, so that wherever they went in the world, they would carry the sense of it with them; so that some near or far eminence with a scatter of houses about its base and trees on its crown would recall that same hill, and their eyes would focus on nothing at all for a few moments of remembering and imagining.

And that is a feeling I have lived with all my life, for I grew up at the foot of just such a hill, albeit in a landscape as different from Mardale Head as you could conceive – on the western edge of Dundee on Scotland's east coast and on the north shore of the Firth of Tay. It was – it still is – called Balgay Hill. It is part woodland and part burial ground, and there lie my parents and three of my grandparents. It was the first of all my landscapes, and whenever I walk there now (no one ever drowned it, so I can still enjoy the privilege), it is the calmest place I know. It lays claim to me. I belong to it. In a very personal book called *The Road and the Miles – A Homage to Dundee* (Mainstream, 1996) I wrote that "although there are more beautiful hills and shores which have seduced my turned back away from Dundee, here is the one place where my own characteristic restlessness likes best to draw breath, and knows it can be briefly still. Here I think only of where I stand, and quietly, I celebrate." I began work on *Lakeland Wild* looking for connections between two landscapes: Lakeland and the landscape to which I belong. As I studied those old photographs, my gaze returned again and again to that singular hill that had been as familiar to the people of Mardale Green as the Balgay Hill was to my young self every time I went to the window or stepped into the garden or walked to and from school, every time I raised my eyes. When I saw that hill in the old photographs of Mardale Green, I found a bridge between landscapes, a bridge I could cross.

Then, one day on my second or third visit to Haweswater, I also found a connection I had not been looking for. It was not another of those connections between two landscapes, but rather one between the Mardale that was a hundred years ago and the Mardale that is today. Staring at one more black and white photograph, I suddenly tumbled to a glaringly obvious truth. In fact, I rebuked myself that the tumbling had taken me so much longer than it should have. The thought that occurred to me sounds absurdly simple now. At the time, it felt like a bit of a breakthrough in my relationship with the Lakeland landscape. That thought was this: they submerged the whole village of "ruptured buildings", but surely there is no way they submerged the whole hill.

So?

So, if you submerge part of a hill but not its summit, what you create instead is an island. The thing had come into my head while I drove south along the shore of Haweswater one quiet morning that coincided with the first warm day of a new spring. I was dawdling on an empty road. I pulled over to watch what I am fairly sure was a newly arrived breeding colony of lesser black-backed gulls. They had staked their claim to the shore and a small area in among the first trees of a compact wooded island. They paired up and squabbled over nest sites and bathed and preened and flashed glossy wings in the sunlight, while their oddly baritone contact calls thermalled up to me. Then my attention wandered from the birds to the wooded island itself. And then it hit me: the gulls are the new community of Mardale Green. And their island home is nothing less than the unsubmerged portion of that hill that adorns so many of the old photographs, in addition to which I came across much more recent colour photographs taken in drought conditions and these revealed the still-indelible autobiography of the lost villagers and their labours, fossilised in old stone. Captions refer to the island as Wood Howe, or sometimes, Wood Howe Island. And I, divining in reverse, had found old land.

The head of Haweswater changed irrevocably from that moment on. I never forgave the reservoir. I shied away from its headwater mountainsides, where summit clouds caught fragments of low sunlight, creating an eerily beautiful species of fiery gloom. I had made tentative plans to explore yet another connection. It was to visit Riggindale, one-time home of the last pair of wild golden eagles in England. I thought something might rub off, given that I have watched golden eagles in Scotland for forty years, on Skye and a smattering of other Hebridean islands, in the Cairngorms, in Angus and Perthshire and Argyll, but mostly in the Stirlingshire portion of the Loch Lomond and the Trossachs National Park, which is both the particular Highland landscape that has adopted me and the one in all Scotland that physically resembles the English Lakes most closely. In fact, Riggindale itself is more like a Highland glen than anywhere else I know in Lakeland. It's hardly surprising. When eagles turned up here again in the 20th century, long after they had been wiped out by the estates, they came from Scotland. Why would they not stake out a valley that most resembled their homeland?

I was struck by the enthusiasm with which the Lakeland eagles' historic presence was still talked about, still signposted, almost celebrated. Odd, I thought, that my brother and I should have had that single, treasured encounter up by Angle Tarn with the male golden eagle that was the last of his line, just before the moment when that line petered out. But the more I thought about Riggindale, the more I thought that the trail of the eagles was cold, that nature had added nothing new to it and so neither could I.

There are straws in the wind, but they make little enough sense. The fledgling South of Scotland Golden Eagle Project, based near Moffat, seeks to consolidate a notoriously fickle golden eagle population by taking chicks from Highland eyries and fledging them in pens in the hills. No one knows how successful this will be yet, and I have always had reservations. I am not convinced that either the habitat or sufficient food source is there, and the Borders' hills have grown an unhelpful crop of hundreds of wind turbines. Yet this seems to be Lakeland's only vision for the return of golden eagles – that a pair might drift south from the Borders. It is hardly an innovative conservation strategy. Alas, for any pair that does make that unlikeliest of moves, the amount of disturbance around the head of Riggindale from the legions that pound along High Street, and the sheer numbers of people who infiltrate almost every corner of Lakeland thanks to its thoughtless tourist industry, pretty well guarantee that no 21st-century golden eagles will linger there. I would be delighted to be proved wrong. But I think Mardale Green will rise from the waves again before eagles nest in Riggindale. Diving in reverse, trying to find old land, only gets harder, whether the land in question is swamped by water boards or tourist boards, and a national park authority that declines to stand up to both.

My exploration of Haweswater's landscape setting began at the far end of the reservoir, trying to park neatly while taking pains to avoid disturbing roadside snowdrops. I liked it already. Nearby, Haweswater Beck emerged – grudgingly it seemed – from *that* dam. In my constant quest for connections, a village called Burnbanks was a bit of a gift for a Scot abroad, perfectly describing its own situation. No one could tell me why it's not called Beckbanks, other than that Burnbanks is a little easier on the ear, a touch more poetic. The irony was not lost on me that even as Mardale Green was being emptied of people then drowned at one end of Haweswater, Burnbanks appeared at the other end for exactly the same reason: that dam. It provided homes for the builders of the dam that would create the reservoir that would drown Mardale Green and change the landscape forever, or for at least as far into the future as any of us can see.

I can't help wondering what else was drowned.

For one thing, I wonder about how much more of Naddle Forest might be down there, crushed and leafless and lifeless beneath the press of water. Step off the narrow cul-de-sac road that leads to Burnbanks today, just before you reach the village, and instantly the world closes in; it has become woody and green and smells of old trees. I first met it in late winter, the snowdrop time. So the pervasive green was not oak foliage but moss. Moss was everywhere. It clung to trunks and limbs and roots, it cloaked boulders in inches-thick living fur. It swarmed over breaking-down and broken-down drystone walls so completely that they seemed to be fashioned from green stones. The oaks – those still living (for this is a wood where dead wood is permitted to lie in state and decompose at its own pace, feeding the soil, nurture for new oaks) – also wore a winter foliage of ferns that crept out along limbs, thickened forks, limpeted up bare trunks. An earthly paradise for nature, you might think, yet it does not suit all the natives.

A treecreeper dived down from the canopy to the base of an oak tree only yards away and immediately set out on its characteristically spiralling ascent of the trunk. It's how they go to work, scouring the bark for its limitless invertebrate life. It is a technique that works beautifully on birch, ash, rowan, aspen, willow…but right here, the bird was immediately constrained by moss. Its huge feet (huge, that is, in the context of a treecreeper – it's the size of a blue tit but its feet are twice the size of a blue tit's) are designed to crampon vertically up bark, not moss. Likewise, its stiff tail, which it angles inwards against the tree as a kind of belay for when its down-curved beak goes hunting from a split-second vertical stance…that tail gets no purchase on plump cushions of moss. But moss hardly ever grows on the south-facing part of a tree trunk, so the treecreeper has had to learn to hunt in zig-zags instead of spirals. It also creeps out along limbs, but then it has ferns to contend with. It must shrug them off as its perpetual motion hunting style wraps the limb in a horizontal spiral. But ferns and moss often grow together, and just as they thicken the trunk on all but its south side, they like the top and sides of limbs but not the underside, so the treecreeper is reduced to hunting along such a limb almost perpetually upside down. It is a bird specifically designed by evolution for a working life on tree bark. In a wood like that one, there must be hundreds of linear miles of the stuff, but a great deal of it is cloaked in moss, and especially on the lower reaches of the trees. If only the treecreeper would stick to the higher reaches of the trees, where the moss peters out and bare bark peters in…but it is also genetically programmed to work a tree from the bottom up. It spirals as far up the tree as it fancies and then flies down to the bottom of an adjacent tree and starts again. I have never seen one start from halfway up the tree. But the rewards of its persistence – that teeming invertebrate life – apparently offered a reward-to-effort ratio sufficient to overwhelm the odds, for the wood was liberally treecreepered. And I suspect that may be the English language's first ever deployment of "treecreeper" as a verb, albeit in the form of a past participle.

Deep in the lowest-lying part of the forest, where a tangible sense of deep green light prevails, there was the nearest thing to the ghost of an oak tree that I have ever seen. At best, you might harvest from what remains a sense of the tree that was; an airy image compiled from a compendium of best guesses. What you can actually see is a wreck. You know those films shot by divers exploring the hull of a casualty of some ancient war on the ocean floor? You get the gist of the vessel that once cleaved the waves in the sun-bright, wind-blown overworld, for all that it now exists only in a state of advanced decrepitude, its hull agape and torn, lit only by the divers' lamps that permit the too-intimate film clips of its sorrows, octopus in the ward room, that kind of thing. The singular oak in Naddle Forest is a kindred spirit, for although in theory it still clings to the surface of the overworld, it is rooted to one of its more Stygian airts where sunlight and wind are piecemeal strangers and the voice of Haweswater Beck adds an appropriately watery undertone. So you confront the shot-to-hell hulk of the oak and your imagination goes to work.

It looks, at first glance, as if three substantial trunks and possibly four have rooted in the top of a low stone wall, until logic kicks in and warns you that such a thing is impossible. Look closer.

The "stone wall" is made of wood and fooled you because it is misshapen and clad in moss, just like the proper stone walls of the wood. What you are seeing are segments of the outer edge of a tree whose trunk must have been seven or eight feet in diameter, a giant, an oaken Goliath. What's left is in two pieces. They face each other across an inner void where the core of the trunk used to be. Each segment is two or three feet thick and the void is four or five feet wide, like an inner courtyard, but one floored by an infinite depth of old leaves and broken pieces of tree in various stages of decomposition. Between them, these two ungainly survivors (liberally blotched and otherwise disfigured with unsightly growths only partly redeemed by their dressings of moss) account for about two-thirds of the circumference of the tree that was. Two drastic breaches permit you to walk right through the tree, although your footing is nowhere secure. The chaos and, frankly, the ugliness of what remains are startlingly fascinating in their own way. You imagine a lightning strike clean through the fork, so unerring in its direction of travel that the vast trunk was sundered to the root. When the dust and the fire settled, and when the corruption and collapse of the tree's inner strength and the stilling of its arboreal heartbeat were achieved, the larger of the two fragmented outcasts that survived (with all the grace of lepers who survived an epidemic) painfully thrust three slender trunks vertically from its own torn roots, a gesture of quite phenomenal futility – for a such a fatally ruinous tree no longer had the resources to sustain its ambition. The trunks still stand, but they bear no fruit, no branch, no twig, no leaf. And perhaps the lesser remnant tried for a trunk, too, for such may have been the broken, rotting spar that still leans against it, submitting silently to the swaddling of moss and the embrace of the woodland floor.

If you walk this way and chance upon the tree, it feels necessary to pay your respects to the final throes of a forest giant. It may feel like a profoundly sad thing to witness, yet even this has its place in nature's scheme of things when it is permitted to look after its own. The space around the ruin is suggestive of the realm it presided over – a girth, a height and a canopy to which every other living thing deferred. Think of how many millions of creatures found sustenance and shelter there in its centuries-long life. Think how many hundreds of thousands of acorns it cast down, how many scattered by wind and bird and squirrel to the depths of the forest so that oaks would prosper, generation on generation on generation. And when the death throes began and the tree began to break down and, at the funeral-march-slow pace of evolution, the eternal processes of renewal started to unfold, untold numbers of life-forms flooded the corpse of the tree and its place in the forest. If you ever wondered what a true miracle actually looks like, it's this.

Such a tree is not just emblematic of a handsome forest, it also symbolises nature's capacity for grand gestures. So when I say of Haweswater Reservoir that I wonder what else was drowned, I'm thinking of forest and the legions of nature's creatures denied that portion of forest for evermore.

One day, years from now, a passing susceptible mortal or two will pause here and ponder over a smooth and low-lying dome of moss that rises from the woodland floor at the heart of a circle of oak saplings, and they might wonder at the events that caused such a thing. For a moment, they might consider the possibility that it was the work of humankind, of some ancient woodland ritual. Or, if they are sufficiently attuned to their surroundings, might they conclude that the low dome of moss is nothing less than a tomb, a burial cairn marking the last resting place of the greatest tree in all Lakeland.

Divining in Reverse

★ ★ ★

A track begins where the metalled road to Burnbanks ends at the far edge of the village, and it follows the west shore of Haweswater all the way to Mardale Head. On a sunny day the walk is awash with light, the water a blank canvas for the sun's dazzle to paint. The reservoir is eel-shaped, its head at the dam and a peculiar fish tail (peculiar for an eel, that is) at Mardale Head. Like Ullswater, its south end falters in the face of a swirl of mountain walls, and for many a walker here, the temptation is to take the beaten track as the be-all-and-end-all and swallow the light-bathed world whole: what I have come to think of as end-to-end syndrome. But I am not made that way. I crave the unbeaten track and the trackless, the off-piste, the hidden landscape, the truly wild wherever it can be found. The national park indulges the walk-this-way culture (I can't help feeling it should be a little more thoughtful), and I shudder at the very language of the culture too. A website sample from a list of "13 walks worthy of world recognition" is suitably wince-inducing: "Scafell Pike, England's highest mountain – Due to demand … we'll be introducing a new guided walk to this peak-bagger's bucket-list must-do." I read that and thought that the peak-bagger with a bucket-list of must-dos and the national park's policy-makers and blurb-writers could benefit from time spent reimagining the landscape of Lakeland.

The track crosses Measand Beck by a waterfall. Its gorge is too steep-sided and rock-hewn for the grazing tribes, so those blood-out-of-a-stone trees that can handle rock and perpetual wetness thrive there. It's a natural photograph pit-stop for the end-to-end bucket-listers, but then the track beckons them on and so does the guidebook. My internal compass is otherwise aligned. Its needle twitches towards the beck itself: this way, it says. Why? Because there is no reason to believe that the fall beside the track is the best of Measand Beck. There is a path of sorts that may have been made by a badger (again!), for there are signs of them all the way down the track from Burnbanks: a substan-tial sett, a latrine, places where they have ducked under a woodland fence and left hairs stuck to the wire, random diggings. The path snakes away uphill. Gone-over bracken licks at its airspace, a pale gold tracery fading towards cold-tea-brown. Eventually, something about the lie of the land seemed to recommend a trackless diversion beneath a buttress, a diversion back towards the beck. Its voice was suddenly louder. Then louder still. One slightly uneasy step prompted a pause to examine a phenomenon: an ash tree that appeared to have swallowed a ten-foot-high, corrupted cube of a rock, an illusion created by the fact that its roots were on the downhill side, its trunk was short and stubby, and it had achieved extraordinary growth by wrapping the boulder with seven substantial limbs and thrusting a canopy, of a kind, out from each one. Tree and rock, you imagine, anchor each other in place. Lakeland is truly a landscape of unique trees.

One more awkward step led out onto a level terrace with just about enough room for two people to sit, a box seat with a view that was all waterfall. There are few things more truly wild in such a landscape than a waterfall hidden from the rest of the world. Whenever you take a chance on an impulse that may or may not bear fruit, there will be times when your reward is the company of nature herself.

It looked from there as if the beck curved then briefly straightened again just above the lip of the fall. A level plain of water fronted a steep background of shrubby, wooded hillside. But unseen from the ledge, the beck bifurcated up there. I only know that because right in front of me, what must have been the right-hand fork breached the wall of the gorge and pounded down over steeply piled rocks to a boisterous reunion with its kindred spirit. A meeting of waterfalls is a portentous place. I have never met a dull one or even an unexceptional one. This one derived much of its spectacle from its seclusion. It was not visible from anywhere other than that moment when you tiptoe past that ash tree with a lump in its throat the size of an elephant, part its overhanging foliage, shrug aside a last irritation of bracken, then a careful boot tests a flat rock for stability because it leans slightly outwards towards an abyss, the reassured boot pivots left, eyes raise, and there it is.

Where the two waterfalls met, there was a broom bush laden with burst-open, autumn-blackened pods, and rooted in a state of perpetual irrigation. The gorge was graced by oak, rowan, gorse (still vividly and richly in broom in early October, for it flowers to one extent or another twelve months of the year) and willow. The beck was two pure colours – deepest black and brightest white, no intermediate shade. The roughly rectangular nature of the rocks and the way such weight of water moved over and among them suggested a slightly haywire three-dimensional chessboard.

A foreground rock struck a jarring note. It thrust forward three razor-edged outcrops that angled back up towards the falls, each of them clad in a carefully painted topcoat of palest green lichen. These reached into space like bowsprits, the green set off by a background of water at its most boisterous, a tumult that derived from the vortex where the two waterfalls collided and rocked the gorge to its foundation.

The bank above the meeting of the falls, a blended chaos of heather, fern, a curtseying willow, gorse and bare rock, wore a momentary flourish of rust-red in a curve that clung to the outermost edge of the bank – effectively a clifftop – and moved with a well-practised assurance. The curve straightened, became a fox. The white tip of its tail wavered and receded upstream towards the only possible destination – the top of the waterfall. The fox vanished in the press of vegetation taller than itself, and left a question unanswered. Did it plan to cross the beck *behind* the waterfall? Otherwise, what was the point of being there? It never reappeared, neither on the far bank nor retracing its steps. But the question only arose in the first place because I have seen it done before. Not here, but in circumstances where the fox chose the waterfall crossing rather than a choice of arguably easier crossings above and below the fall. But "easier" is a human judgement. It's what you or I would choose, and the fox had its own reasons for its choice. One could have been that the waterfall crossing was more discreet. Another could have been that the fox enjoyed the waterfall option, enjoyed the unique space between water and rock where the fall billowed out and left an agreeably moist and airy and cool route on a hot day, a route that would also confound its enemies.

I don't know if the Measand Beck fox crossed by the fall. I don't have to know. I like to think it did, simply because the possibility occurred to me and I hold that possibility as the crowning event of the moments I shared with the fall. But I also like it when nature stays my hand and leaves me a mystery for a souvenir, something to mull over months and years from now, when I am far from here and see a fox move in a way that suggests that confident curve on the clifftop above the fall and my mind's eye travels back here again. When that happens, I choose to believe that nature knows what it's doing. That day at Measand Beck, the fox added a grace note to the song of that place.

★ ★ ★

Remember this?

> ...*In all shapes*
> *He found a secret and mysterious soul,*
> *A fragrance and a spirit of strange meaning.*

Wordsworth again. And that word "soul" is in the air again. I am agnostic in the matter of the soul, borderline atheist. Otherwise, I could make a case for that hidden meeting of waterfalls as a glimpse of Lakeland's soul. But surely, it is in the nature of souls that they cannot be glimpsed? What I think of as my essential earth-rootedness inclines me away from the spiritual and towards the physical, so a pulse, perhaps, or a heartbeat the dam-builders and their imposed–on–the–land lake can neither still nor silence. All I know is that a key turned for me here, and for a moment I had found old land again. And these mountain waters like Measand Beck are the true headwaters of Haweswater Beck and they always have been.

Old Land.
Old Waters.
Lakeland Wild.

Acknowledgements

My debt of gratitude to those who have assisted the cause of this book begins with my publisher, Sara Hunt, of Saraband. Quite simply, it was her idea. So thanks, Sara, you were right again.

Another key factor in deciding to act on her suggestion was a grant from Creative Scotland, which covered the costs of travel and accommodation, and helped me to make sense of the whole project. Once again, I found the staff at Creative Scotland very professional and helpful and very easy to deal with. Thank you for easing my path into a project that has allowed me to push my nature writing into new directions, both geographically and creatively.

No one can travel far in Lakeland without rubbing up against the twin legacies of William Wordsworth and A.W. Wainwright. My early determination to give them both as wide a berth as possible soon evaporated. My thanks to all who cherish their legacies. In particular, Jonathan Bate's literary biography, *Radical Wordsworth,* was a timely publication and opened doors for me into Wordsworth's writing mind.

What cheered me as a Scot with the temerity to write about Lakeland was the discovery of the role of Robert Burns in shaping Wordsworth's writing. Not the least of the qualms that I had about writing this book in the first place was a revelation in Robert Crawford's biography of Burns, *The Bard*. His fellow Scottish poet, Don Paterson, told him he would be writing "the world's least necessary book". A thought crossed my mind when I read that at absolutely the wrong time: "Apart from maybe a new book about the Lake District." There again, Robert Crawford wrote his book anyway and I read it.

You will gather from the text of *Lakeland Wild* that, in general, I am not a fan of guidebooks. A 50th-anniversary set of Wainwright's seven *Pictorial Guides to the Lakeland Fells* now sits on my bookshelves, the solitary exception to my ambivalence. I never once consulted them to choose a route, but I *read* them, and I still do. These seven have become the beginning and the end of my guidebook selection.

The American nature-writing tradition is one I have admired and devoured for many years now. What took me by surprise was a sub-plot that emerged in *Lakeland Wild* that led me from Wordsworth's doorstep via Emerson, Thoreau, Whitman, Muir and Leopold straight to my own doorstep. The tradition of nature writing in which I am immersed owes much to that remarkable lineage, and to the miraculous flowering of American nature writing in the late 20th and early 21st centuries. I am unquestionably one of its beneficiaries.

One of that literary tradition's giants, Barry Lopez, died at Christmas 2020, as I was writing the final chapters of *Lakeland Wild*. As one with an all-encompassing passion for the north of this planet, it is hard for me to overstate the impact of reading *Arctic Dreams* for the first time, and then, ten years later, finding a lovely American first edition

Acknowledgements

of it in a bookshop in Juneau, Alaska. That book crossed the Atlantic with me and is one of the most thumbed and admired and wondered at of all my books.

Others American writers whose work has been summoned to this book's cause are David M. Carroll (*Self-Portrait with Turtles*) and Fred Hagender (*The Spirit of Trees*).

The landscape of Lakeland has not so much a literary tradition all of its own, rather it has a literary avalanche. I am grateful in particular to Sarah Hall's novel, *Haweswater*, which allowed me an understanding of the impact of the reservoir on both the human population and the landscape. And W.R. Philipson's relatively unsung but intriguing nature-writing period piece from the early 1940s, *Birds of a Valley*, fell into my lap by a happy accident, the valley in question being that of Goldrill Beck.

A special word of thanks to a friend of many years, David Craig. David is a fellow Scot, long domiciled in Burton-in-Kendal, retired professor of creative writing at the University of Lancaster, a writer of distinction in fiction, non-fiction and poetry, much of it rooted in landscape. The book I have borrowed from here, with his whole-hearted permission, is *Native Stones – A Book About Climbing*, much of which draws on rock climbs across the north of England, but in his sure hands it is rock-climbing rendered as literature. It was the first book of his that I read, and his work has been an inspiration to me ever since. We have shared memorable times together in landscapes as diverse as his local limestone pavement, the Moine Mhor in the high Cairngorms, Balquhidder Glen in the Loch Lomond and the Trossachs National Park and the islands of Pabay, Mingulay and Barra.

Others whose work I have referenced in gratitude and admiration are Seton Gordon (again!), Gavin Maxwell, Marion Campbell, Margiad Evans, foresters H.M. Steven and A. Carlisle, Hugh Johnson, C.F. Tunnicliffe, and the mighty Scottish bard who some say is the best since Burns, Hugh MacDiarmid. Blessings on all their shades, and I am grateful forever that their work outlives them.

Another great friend who continues to stalk through my life and work a decade after his death, George Garson, is here too, for his insights into the work of painter Paul Nash.

Two unlikely sources gave me food for thought and helped me to unearth unsuspected treasures. The first was the School of Forestry at the University of Cumbria, whose conference report of 2012, which I stumbled across online, led me directly to Young Wood, which is a kind of silvicultural miracle. The second was Stirling GP Dr Ian Hanley who digressed during a consultation to enlighten me about schellies, about which I previously knew nothing at all.

Each time I reach this point in writing the manuscript of a book, it has become a bit of a tradition to thank three people who collectively form a substantial part of my writing's life-support system. They are publisher Sara Hunt (see above!); Craig Hillsley, editor of this and all my other Saraband books and who repeatedly justifies my oft-uttered maxim that good editors are worth their weight in gold; and literary agent Jenny Brown who is just the very best in the business.

Finally, permit me to honour a friend of nearer fifty years than forty who died while I was working on this book, and to whom the book is dedicated. He was Keith Graham, retired countryside ranger, cricketer and wildlife writer. We shared so many wildlife adventures, and so many glasses of good whisky (of which he was something of a connoisseur) and some of the best Hogmanays of my life. He was born in Manchester, the passion of his young life was the Lakeland fells, and he was the first person I ever heard articulate a passion for them. But Keith's ancestry was rooted in the old Stirlingshire parish of Menteith, which he visited often as a boy on family holidays. In the mid-1970s he landed his dream job, to set up the Stirling District countryside ranger service, which in turn allowed him to live at Port of Menteith, and there he spent the rest of his life.

I interviewed him when he arrived, for at the time I was the editor of the *Stirling Observer*. One of the first fruits of what very quickly became a friendship was that Keith began writing a weekly wildlife column for the paper. It was called "Country View". I left the paper after three years, but Keith's column was still going after forty-seven years. The week he died, he had begun his latest column but hadn't finished it. He never missed a deadline. His family saw to it that he didn't miss that one. Over the years there were three published collections of his column. The very first one is beside me as I write this, and I have just reacquainted myself, not just with Keith's writing, but also with the short foreword that I wrote for it:

You won't find Keith Graham's country views from the window of a car. You will find them ankle deep in the treacheries of Flanders Moss where an otter betrays himself in a square inch of mud.

You will find them cramped and shivering after a motionless vigil at a badger sett. You will find them by a shimmering unsuspected lochan, folded neatly away in the Menteith Hills. You will find his watcher's eye and his listener's ear will open your own eyes and ears, as they have done for countless readers of his weekly column in the Stirling Observer, *as they have done for me.*

JIM CRUMLEY HAS WRITTEN forty-one books, mostly on the wildlife and wild landscape of his native Scotland, the impact of human activity on the natural world, species reintroduction, and climate change. His work has been shortlisted for prestigious awards including the Wainwright Prize, the Highland Prize and the Saltire Society Literary Awards. Jim is a widely published journalist and has a monthly column in *The Scots Magazine*, as well as being a poet and occasional broadcaster on both radio and television.

Lakeland Wild

Also by Jim Crumley

The Nature of Summer
The Nature of Spring
The Nature of Winter
The Nature of Autumn
Nature's Architect
The Eagle's Way
Encounters in the Wild series:
Fox, Barn Owl, Swan, Hare,
Skylark, Badger, Kingfisher, Otter

The Great Wood
The Last Wolf
The Winter Whale
Brother Nature
Something Out There
The Mountain of Light
Gulfs of Blue Air
The Company of Swans
Among Mountains
Among Islands
The Road and the Miles
Waters of the Wild Swan
Shetland – Land of the Ocean
A High and Lonely Place
St Kilda